ONCE THERE WAS AN AMERICA

LT. COLONEL (RET) BILL A. HEATON

Best Wishes

Bill A. Heaton

The opinions expressed in this manuscript are solely the opinions of the author and do not represent the opinions or thoughts of the publisher. The author has represented and warranted full ownership and/or legal right to publish all the materials in this book.

Once There Was An America
All Rights Reserved.
Copyright © 2012 Lt. Colonel (Ret) Bill A. Heaton
v3.0

Cover Photo © 2012 JupiterImages Corporation. All rights reserved - used with permission.

This book may not be reproduced, transmitted, or stored in whole or in part by any means, including graphic, electronic, or mechanical without the express written consent of the publisher except in the case of brief quotations embodied in critical articles and reviews.

Outskirts Press, Inc.
http://www.outskirtspress.com

ISBN: 978-1-4327-9222-0

Outskirts Press and the "OP" logo are trademarks belonging to Outskirts Press, Inc.

PRINTED IN THE UNITED STATES OF AMERICA

Dedicated to my wife, Linda
For her patience and assistance.

Contents

1 How Our Downfall Began 1
2 Early Gains Toward World Control 10
3 The Federal Reserve System 23
4 Immigration And Labor Unions 35
5 The American Civil Liberties Union 55
6 The Constitution of the United States of America 63
7 Socialism, Communism, and Leftism In America 100
8 Socialism In The United States Education System 117
9 The Council On Foreign Relations 129
10 The Trilateral Commission 148
11 The United Nations and the Mainstream Media 156
12 The Obama Tragedy 167
13 Taking Back America 187
Notes 205

CHAPTER 1

How Our Downfall Began

ONCE THERE WAS an America. To the real, the true, the correctly informed, the patriotic, freedom-loving, "previous" Americans, these are the saddest words ever heard.

Throughout its existence no rational authority has denied the fact that the United States of America was the greatest and most influential nation known to mankind. The great world empires and dynasties throughout recorded history all paled in comparison to this new and wonderful country.

The following pages will not concentrate on the early Colonial days of our country. However, they will cover important facts and events from the beginning of the eighteenth century to the middle and latter parts of the twentieth century when the United States reached its zenith. Additionally, I will pick up the unknown and accelerated beginning of our downfall in the early and middle part of the twentieth century and how we lost our country through apathy and Fabian (creeping) Socialism, with the climax occurring in November 2008. As a result, we are simply a Socialist country in North America. Finally, I will show how we can reclaim our country and return it to the lofty status it once occupied.

Surely the academic community, the strongly biased mainstream news media, and citizens in general will disagree with my statement that we lost our country in November 2008. This is because their concept of Socialism is the standard definition: [1] "Socialism is a theory or system of social organization in which the means of production and distribution of goods are owned and controlled by the government."

My! How narrow of a view can you get? Socialism means so much more than a mere dictionary definition. A large portion of it is intentionally masked. In the country in which we now live (previously America), we have so many social welfare and political programs that it would take volumes to list and explain all of them. Nevertheless, we will take a look at a few of such programs.

As of January 1, 2011, one-sixth of the United States economy is owned by Obamacare, thirty percent of our banking industry is government-owned, and thirty to thirty-five percent of the auto manufacturing industry is government-owned. Then, we can toss in housing assistance, education assistance, welfare assistance (many families of three generations have been on welfare without single family member ever working at a legally paying job), Supplemental Security Income (SSI), food stamps, daycare assistance, school meals, and the redistribution of wealth through higher and unfair taxes with ongoing efforts to further increase taxes on high earners – an Obama-appointed Czar with a Socialist background is to determine the salaries of corporate executives. These programs will be downplayed by Leftist radicals who call them entitlements and vote-hungry politicians who call them humanitarian efforts. To the realist-thinking, well-informed citizen, this is SOCIALISM no matter what it may be called.

Even before the United States gained her independence from England in 1776, evil and greedy eyes were already focused on this new land with its vast amount of natural resources and many more resources yet to be discovered and developed.

Immediately upon gaining our independence from England, actions in Europe were in a "gear up" mode to gain control of America. Thanks to their intelligence, foresight, common sense, and belief in God, our forefathers forged the most important and most magnificent document known to the world: The United States Constitution.

HOW OUR DOWNFALL BEGAN ➤

Using this fabulous document for approximately one hundred and twenty-five years, courageous and patriotic American leaders were able to ward off most, but not all, of the efforts to these lurking and evil powers from gaining a strong foothold in our government and society.

Most readers will wonder what evil powers I am writing about. This I well understand because I felt the same way in 1964 when I first started studying this subject while stationed in Europe. So, coming directly to the answer, I am referring to the Order of The Illuminati – meaning the enlightened or those who have seen the light.

In addition, readers will probably ask the valid question, "What the heck is that?" Although a huge amount of valid research has been done and many books have been written on The Illuminati, probably less than one percent of the United States population has heard of it. Why is this so? Because The Illuminati began in Bavaria as a small secret society. As time went by, it developed many tentacles that infiltrated all permanent and influential organizations, institutions, and governments. Naturally, The Illuminati did not want its intentions known until it was so powerful that any and all nations would be powerless against it.

Within the last fifteen to twenty years, The Illuminati has been more open, but it and its tentacles seldom use the true name. Now it has become so strong that it openly speaks of its primary objective, which is world control through ownership of the international monetary system. When you see such familiar names as The New World Order, One World Government, An International Trade Economy, An International Government, etc., you are seeing the tentacles of The Illuminati.

As alluded to earlier, The Illuminati controls our government, an overwhelming majority of our "key" politicians, manufacturing, banking, trade unions, other financial institutions, and mainstream media. It also has a strong influence over our religious institutions, motion picture industry, military services, etc. In short, it controls every aspect of our lives. This will become clearer in the following chapters.

◄ ONCE THERE WAS AN AMERICA

Take a bit of time and research a few of The Illuminati's tentacles which may be familiar to you. Organizations such as The Trilateral Commission, The Council on Foreign Relations, Cecil Rhodes (Rhodes Scholarships) and The Round Table, The Bilderberg Group, The Global Elite, The Shadow Government and The Bloodlines of The Illuminati. In your research you will find much of the information favoring these organizations which are written as a cover-up. In order to get to the truth, you must look at the other information which exposes them for what they are actually.

I will not spend more time than necessary on The Illuminati since it requires thousands of pages and you can obtain well-written and well-researched books on the subject. However, you must be careful and open-minded. Most information you find will favor or glorify these tentacles as Pro-American when they actually are not. You will find the truth in books and articles that are considered conservative and published by small publishing houses or self-publishers. Yes! You guessed it: the major publishing firms are controlled by the evil of which I speak. Also, be careful of books that espouse hate, racial prejudice and Anti-Semitism.

Now that we have delved into The Illuminati, it is best that we go back to its beginning. Quoting from Wikipedia the Free Encyclopedia, [2] "Adam Weishaupt (February 6, 1748 in Ingolstadt; November 18, 1838 in Gotha) was a German philosopher and founder of The Order of The Illuminati, a secret society with origins in Bavaria."

At age five, Weishaupt was introduced to the philosophy of the Enlightenment espoused by Professor Christian Wolff. At age seven, Weishaupt began his formal education at a Jesuit school and later enrolled at the University of Ingolstadt, graduating in 1768 with a Doctorate of law and becoming a professor of law in 1772. In 1773, Pope Clement XIV suppressed the Society of Jesus (Jesuits) and Weishaupt became a professor of canon law, a position exclusively held by the Jesuits until that time.

On May 1, 1776, Weishaupt formed the Order of Professionals (The Illuminati). Within the Order, he adopted the name of Brother

HOW OUR DOWNFALL BEGAN

Spartacus, although the Order was not egalitarian or democratic. Its mission was the abolishment of all monarchial governments and state religions in European countries and their colonies.

In 1777, Weishaupt joined the Masonic Lodge in Munich. His efforts of illumination – enlightening the understanding of reason, which would dispel the clouds of superstition and prejudice – were an unwanted reform. However, Weishaupt had developed Gnostic (heretical) mystics of his own. His goal was to perfect human nature through reeducation to achieve a communal state with nature that was free of government, and incorporating The Illuminati with that of Freemasonry.

Weishaupt's radical rationalism and vocabulary were doomed to fail. By an act of God in 1784, a messenger and his horse carrying writings and plans of world control were struck by lightning and killed. These writings and a variety of other documents were seized by government officials who interpreted them as seditious. The Society was banned by the government of Karl Theodore, Elector of Bavaria. As a result, Weishaupt lost his position at the University of Ingolstadt and fled Bavaria.

Weishaupt lived in Gotha until his death on November 18, 1830. Despite his failed efforts from 1784 until his death, Weishaupt continued to gain followers, wrote a series of books on The Illuminati, and developed many tentacles differing slightly from his original work. Most tentacles kept the main character of The Illuminati with a network of spies and counter-spies. Each isolated cell of new members reported to a superior, the identity of whom they did not know.

Weishaupt's recruitment of the intellectuals of his time was far reaching. For example, John Robison, a member of the Freemasons who taught natural philosophy at Scotland's Edinburgh University, was solicited for membership in The Illuminati. After studying the intent, structure, etc., Robison decided that he wanted no part of it. In 1798, he (Robison) published a book called "Proofs of a Conspiracy" wherein he stated, [3] "An association has been formed for the expressed purpose of rooting out all the religious establishments and overturning all existing governments – the leaders would rule the world with uncontrollable power, while the rest would be employed as tools of the ambition of their unknown Superiors."

Robison's book was written very late in his life and he contends that the plans for the World Order were carried on in secret meetings of The Illuminati, Freemasonry and Reading Societies. Independently, French priest Abbe Barruel and Robison developed very similar views that The Illuminati had infiltrated Continental Freemasonry and especially the manipulation of the Rothschild Banking System bringing about the French Revolution, which was financed on both sides by Rothschild (more on the Rothschild later).

The title of Robison's book was "Proofs of a Conspiracy Against all the Religions and Governments of Europe." In 1798, the Reverend G.W. Snyder sent a copy of Robison's book to George Washington for his thoughts on the subject. On October 24, 1798, George Washington wrote in reply to Reverend Snyder, "It was not my intention to doubt that, the doctrine of The Illuminati and principles of Jacobinism have not spread in the United States. On the contrary, no one is more truly satisfied of this fact than I am. The idea that I mean to convey, was, that I did not believe that the Lodges of Masons in the country had, as societies, endeavored to propagate the diabolical tenets of the first, or promiscuous principles of the latter (if they are susceptible of separation)."

It is evident that George Washington had early knowledge of The Illuminati's plan to establish a World Order. In a joint session of Congress, President Washington warned all members of the evil intent of The Illuminati and stated that each member should denounce this cabal. I find it interesting because sitting across from him was Thomas Jefferson, who was already a member of The Illuminati and had this to say of Weishaupt, [4] "An enthusiastic philanthropist. He is among those who believe in the indefinite probability of man. He thinks he may in time be rendered so perfect that he will be able to govern himself in every circumstance."

More modern conspiracy theorists such as Nesta Helen Webster

HOW OUR DOWNFALL BEGAN ▶

and William Guy Carr, Commander in the Royal Canadian Navy believe that Robison's book describes that what The Illuminati may have started was the model for the subversion of benign organizations by radical groups throughout the nineteenth and twentieth centuries, especially in the United States. "Spiritual Counterfeits" author, Tal Brooke, believes that the views written by Robison and those of Carol Quigley's "Tragedy and Hope" (Macmillan 1966) are comparable. Brooke also believes that The New World Order which Adam Weishaupt started will now be completed with the power of international bankers led by the Rothschild's (more later), The Federal Reserve System, The International Monetary Fund and The World Bank.

At this point, for the purpose of clarity, we need to regress to the approximate period of 1774-1775. During this period, Weishaupt and a young banker named Mayer Amschel Rothschild began a close association due to their shared views of world control. I again refer to his book, [5] "Pawns in the Game" (1954) wherein Commander William Guy Carr, an Intelligence Officer in the Royal Canadian Navy, who had excellent contacts in intelligence circles around the world, found that Mayer Rothschild drew up the plans for the creation of The Illuminati and then entrusted Adam Weishaupt with its organization and development. This scheme allowed Mayer Rothschild to pursue his purpose of world control through the international banking system, while at the same time Weishaupt was carrying on activities that enhanced Rothschild's scheme, yet diverted attention from it. Both Weishaupt and Rothschild agreed that a plan for world control had to be accomplished very gradually and there would be gains and setbacks over time. Gains were greater over more than two centuries ago until the culmination in 2008. Now it is time to take a closer look at Mayer Amschel Rothschild.

[6] Mayer Amschel Rothschild was born February 23, 1744 in Frankfurt, Germany and died September 19, 1812. He was born and grew up in a ghetto called Judengass or Jew Alley. Mayer's father had a business in the trade of small goods and currency exchange that

aroused Mayer's interest in banking. Mayer was given an apprenticeship in the banking firm of Jakob Wolf in Hamburg, Germany. After his apprenticeship, he returned to Frankfurt in 1763.

Mayer became a dealer in rare coins and won the favor of Crown Prince William of Hesse and gained the title of Court Factor. With a shrewd and conniving mind, he grew his business so as to include man princely patrons. He never hesitated in sucking up to anyone who could help him in his quest for power. By the early years of the nineteenth century, Mayer had consolidated his position as principal international banker to Wilhelm IX, Landgrave of Hesse. At this time, he began making his own international loans, borrowing capital from the Landgrave. This was his first step in developing the House of Rothschild, also known as the Rothschild Dynasty.

Mayer Amschel Rothschild was a hard-hearted man without scruples, doing anything from providing "human flesh" (troops for armies) to financing both sides of nations at war. I am purposefully skipping over most of the ruthlessness of Mayer in his pursuit of world control. I suggest you obtain and read a copy of [7] Des Griffin's book "Descent into Slavery." In his book, Griffin goes into a masterful, in-depth study of this subject. You may also use your computer simply by researching The Rothschild Dynasty and you will find a condensed version of Chapter Five of Mr. Griffin's book.

Before leaving Mayer Rothschild, I will point out how he initially expanded his banking dynasty and gained control of the industry in Europe. In 1798, he began dispensing his sons to establish banking control over centers in key cities throughout Europe, as follows:

1. Nathaniel was sent to London to establish his first foreign bank.
2. Amschel was in charge of the Berlin Branch.
3. Solomon established the family bank in Vienna.
4. Jacob (James) went to Paris where the bank flourished.
5. Kalman (Karl) set up shop in Naples.

Note: the headquarters of the House of Rothschild was, and is, in London.

HOW OUR DOWNFALL BEGAN

The Illuminati/Rothschild Dynasty is so complex that it is almost impossible to explain. Its tentacles are many, interlocking, and often apparently opposing each other. This is done to confuse and hinder our knowledge of their true meaning. Additionally, new tentacles are constantly being added as nation and world conditions change.

In all of the foregoing facts, I simply have tried to give you a small background in order for you to understand how we got into the awful state of affairs in which the United States now finds itself. It will become clearer in following chapters. Moreover, you must always remember that most events which happen, whether they are economical, political, educational, or entry into war, are the product of the cabal. And, every aspect of your life is influenced and frequently controlled by it Also remember events which take place in present times were planned many years prior and are only now occurring since all aspects of the conquest were based on gradualism (creeping Socialism) or waiting until time and conditions are right for implementation.

It has often been said that wherever a mark, a franc, a pound, or a dollar can be made, a Rothschild or a Rothschild agent will be there to take advantage and obtain the largest share.

Following the French Revolution, while handling payments from Britain for the Hussein mercenaries, Mayer learned that there was big money to be made in war. From that time to the present, the Rothschild Dynasty has helped in promoting war and on more than one occasion has financed both sides of the war. This includes the War Between the States in America. This will be discussed in greater detail in a later chapter.

CHAPTER 2

Early Gains Toward World Control

AS SEEN IN the preceding chapter, Mayer Rothschild had solidified the Rothschild's position as the leader of the international banking establishment with control in England, Germany, France, Austria, and Italy. The Rothschild Dynasty not only continues to hold this position in Europe, it holds the position throughout the world and especially in the United States. Naturally, all other international bankers follow their lead in practically all major decisions.

From this point forward I will, when practical, I will refrain from using the phrase "The Rothschild's" or "The Rothschild Dynasty" or the "International Bankers." Instead, I will use the term "The Evil Octopus," because tentacles are often grown or added when needed. However, from time to time, I will remind you that The Evil Octopus is the International Bankers.

We already know that evil, covetous, and conniving eyes were cast toward the United States, but immediately upon establishing himself as the leader among the International Bankers, Mayer Rothschild made vigorous efforts toward a foothold in the new and prosperous nation which he considered the greatest prize of all.

We made detest his greed and ruthless tactics but must give credit for his knowledge and guile that was necessary for his method of success. He well knew that it took money to make more money. Accordingly, he set up a network of agents and spies in the United

EARLY GAINS TOWARD WORLD CONTROL

States before he made his first move into American affairs.

The International Bankers were frustrated in their efforts to establish a central bank in America. We were a unique nation whose government was formed with the Bible as its law book that guided our Christian founding fathers in writing the United States Constitution which is still considered the most magnificent document ever written. The establishment of a Constitutional Republic (not a democracy) with the powers equally divided among three branches: The Executive, The Legislative, and The Judicial were more difficult to manipulate than the Monarchies of Europe. Despite their frustrations, the International Bankers sent a multitude of financial agents to America whose efforts were to seek a means of establishing a central bank to be owned and controlled by European Bankers.

Another obstacle in the efforts of the International Bankers establishing a central bank in the United States was that most of our founding fathers, and practically all of our citizens, were leery of banks in general and central banks in particular. Our immigrant citizens who had come to have the freedom of religion, to be free as individuals, to have the opportunity to work, and to enjoy the fruits of their labor had seen the evil and ruthless power of the central banks in Europe. Our political leaders had not yet become corrupt and strongly remembered that England tried to place the Colonies under the monetary control of the Bank of England. Despite these facts, the International Bankers made some headway into our early banking system during the following periods:

    1781-1836 – First Bank of the United States
                Second Bank of the United States
    1837-1864 – The "Free Banking Era"
    1836-1913 – National Banks
    1907-1913 – The movement to create the Federal Reserve System

We will come back to the above periods of banking for details on each period. You will have to hang with me because we will be going

◄ ONCE THERE WAS AN AMERICA

backward and forward in time since some periods overlap. Important events occurred between periods and we will be discussing several important banking individuals of the period.

In studying the history of banking in the United States, we must remember there was always some form of banking going on, but the big names in banking were Jewish. This is simply a historical fact and in no way do I espouse any form of Anti-Semitism. You will also see that the German-Jewish bankers were a close-knit group who supported each other and collectively worked toward the creation of a central bank. To emphasize the closeness of the group at this time, intermarriage among the German-Jewish elite was customary.

One of the Rothschild's earlier financial agents in the United States who was used in their first known involvement in the financial affairs of America was Nicholas Biddle.

Nicholas Biddle was an arrogant, pompous, well-educated and intelligent individual, who in today's society would be called a highly intelligent nerd. As a child, he chose not to play with other children or engage in any child-like activities. Instead, he chose to read and become self-educated. At age ten, Biddle entered the University of Pennsylvania in 1796. During his junior or senior year, he was notified that he would not be awarded his degree because of his age. Biddle then enrolled in the sophomore class at Princeton, where he later graduated.

At age nineteen, Biddle was invited to work as an unpaid secretary in Paris for General John Armstrong. During his stay in Paris he became associated with the International Bankers and gained a vast amount of knowledge on international finance. He then went to London, spent time with James Monroe, and gained more knowledge of international banking.

Biddle's time in Europe was exceedingly rewarded. The Rothschild's recognized his potential and hired him as an agent. While serving in the Pennsylvania House of Representatives, James Monroe appointed him as a director of the Second Bank of the United States in 1819. Three years later he became the president of the bank

EARLY GAINS TOWARD WORLD CONTROL

until it went out of business in 1836.

Although the Rothschild and Nicholas Biddle were accomplished veterans of international banking, they could not match an old warhorse like Andrew Jackson. The Rothschild provided Biddle with advice and a plethora of money to fight and defeat President Jackson's move to diminish the power of the bank. President Jackson considered International Bankers lower than snakes and vetoed the move to renew the charter of the Bank of the United States, forcing it to close in 1836.

Extremely huge strides had been made in the United States by the International Bankers in establishing their own banks and gaining strong control or influence over other banks. This was not nearly enough for the Rothschild Dynasty; therefore, the next attempt by the Rothschild's into the financial affairs of the United States came prior to and during the War Between the States.

[1] A strong relationship had developed between the cotton barons of the South and the textile manufacturers in England prior to the War Between the States. To a smaller degree, this type of relationship was also developed with other European nations. When hostilities began in 1861, it was assumed by many concerned nations and individuals that England would join with the South in its war with the North. Much can be written on this subject but I will cut it short by saying it just never happened due to circumstances we will later discuss.

The Rothschild wanted to destroy the United States by dividing America into two opposing nations whereby the International Bankers could continually pit one against the other, as they had done with the European nations. They had agents who were American citizens, who worked both sides and encouraged the split of America. They provided financial backing, armaments, and even the intervention of European armies and naval power.

Many researchers claim the Rothschild financed both the North and the South during the War Between the States. In my many years of study, I have not been able to prove this to my own satisfaction. [2] We do know with certainty that President Lincoln refused to pay the extremely high interest rate charged by the Rothschild's and other International Bankers and issued interest-free United States Notes.

Fearing that England would enter the war in support of the South, President Lincoln appealed to Czar Nicholas II of Russia for assistance. [3] During the winter of 1861-1862, the Imperial Russian Navy sent two fleets to the United States. Despite the fact that England made it clear that she would not enter the war, the Alexander Nevsky and other vessels of the Russian Atlantic Squadron stayed in American waters for seven more months.

According to many theorists, the International Bankers were so enraged over the two foregoing actions by President Lincoln that they arranged for his assassination by John Wilkes Booth on April 14, 1865 at Ford's Theater. This was only a few days after General Robert E. Lee surrendered the Confederate Army at the Appomattox Court House in Virginia.

Many of the above theories came from John Wilkes Booth's Granddaughter Idola Forrester. [4] Mrs. Forrester (November 15, 1878 – March 6, 1944) was a highly successful newspaper and magazine journalist and editor. She was the author of more than twenty books and later was a successful screenwriter. She and her husband, playwright Mann Page, Jr. (common law marriage) had thirty six films from the silent eras: "The Quitter" (1915) starring Lionel Barrymore to the talkies "She Had to Choose" (1934) starring Buster Crabbe (I saw him in an early Tarzan movie and several Grade B westerns). They also collaborated with Douglas Fairbanks and Sinclair Lewis.

[5] In Idola Forrester's last book, "This One Mad Act: The Unknown Story of John Wilkes Booth by His Granddaughter" (1934), she writes of her childhood memories of her mother's and grandmother's connection with John Wilkes Booth. She states that Booth had been in contact with European bankers prior to the killing of President Lincoln. She also states that Booth was hastily carried away by members of a secret society known as The Sons of Liberty, previously known as the Knights of the Golden Circle. This was the second reorganization of the secret society formed in Ohio and later moved to the South.

EARLY GAINS TOWARD WORLD CONTROL ▶

According to Mrs. Forrester, John Wilkes Booth lived under an assumed name for many years following his disappearance.

Earlier in this chapter I promised to go back to four periods in American Banking and discuss some important bank officials of the times. We will uncover the first three periods but we will not cover the fourth until Chapter Three. This period (1907-1913) is extremely important and deserves exceptional and diligent effort to show how the Federal Reserve System was created, why it was created in such a clandestine manner, and who profited and continues to profit from it. Practically all of you will be amazed with the facts we will uncover in the study of this subject.

[6] Nearly every country around the world and certainly every developed industrial nation has a central bank. Most serve one or more of the following functions: acting as a bank for bankers, issuing a common currency, clearing payments, regulating banks and acting as a "lender of last resort" for banks in financial trouble. The one thing they all do is serve as banker to their own government.

Most central banks have common practices yet they operate in distinctive ways which usually comes from the bank's historical background. To understand that nature of a central bank, you have to study its history and relationship to commerce and government. The unique structure of the United States Federal Reserve System makes this especially true since the shaping was done from the past experience of trying to establish a central bank. Another extremely large factor was the influence of foreign interest (capital) in establishing our central bank.

1791-1836 – The First and Second Banks of the United States:

The United States found itself in substantial debt as the result of the Revolutionary War. To finance the war, the Continental Congress printed the nation's first paper money known as "Continentals." Originally the notes were intended to be redeemed on demand in specie (gold or silver). Instead, the Congress reneged on its promise and issued notes in such high quantity that they led to inflation which continually increased to the point where people lost total faith in the notes. This is where the phrase "not worth a continental" came into being, meaning "completely worthless." Faced with this problem, President George Washington directed Alexander Hamilton, the Secretary of the Treasury to establish the First Bank of the United States which was conceived in 1790.

As the architect, Alexander Hamilton modeled the bank after the Bank of England. Naturally, Hamilton had a massive amount of obstacles to overcome into which we will not go. The bank was intended to help fund the government's debt, issue currency notes, and, in general, put the country on sound financial footing.

Plans were laid for the First Bank of the United States to have start-up capital of ten million dollars to be obtained by selling stock. The United States government would own two million dollars which later proved to be insufficient since the remaining eighty percent was owned by private investors that primarily consisted of the Rothschild and other International Bankers. The main office was located in Philadelphia and one of eight branches was in each of the nation's major cities. Here we can see the influence of the International Bankers with the bank being the forerunner of the Federal Reserve System. Naturally, there was bitter opposition by several founding fathers, including Thomas Jefferson and James Monroe, who saw it as a driving force for financial manipulation, speculation, and corruption.

We can confidently say the First Bank of the United States had a fair amount of success. It succeeded in paying off the Revolutionary War debt and was successful in its commercial operations. From its initial planning, the bank was opposed by those critics who agreed that it was unconstitutional. This was a strong argument since the United States Constitution grants power to tax, print, and coin money to Congress and certainly not to a private corporation. When the bank's charter came up for renewal in 1811, Congress refused and the bank ceased operations.

The Second Bank of the United States:

Much like the First Bank of the United States, the government was faced with a large debt caused by the War of 1812. Combined with war debt, state-chartered banks were issuing their own currency. These banks then suspended specie (gold and silver) payments. As a result, public opinion again became favorable to the idea of a central bank.

The Second National Bank was almost a copy of the First Bank, but somewhat larger. It had a capital of thirty-five million with the United States government-owning one-fifth. It also had its headquarters in Philadelphia. Before its demise, the Second Bank had offices in twenty-nine major cities.

As discussed earlier, Nicholas Biddle, who was the chief agent of the Rothschild, began using the bank's resources against President Andrew Jackson. President Jackson had always considered (rightfully so) the International Bankers as a den of snakes. So, in 1832, he refused to renew the Bank's Charter and it simply withered away until the charter expired in 1836.

1837-1862 – "Free Banking Era":

There had previously been state-chartered banks; however, the loss of the Second Bank of the United States created a need for more banks. [7] During the period from 1837 to the War Between the States, commonly known as the "Free Banking Era," states passed free banking laws which allowed banks to operate under a much less onerous charter.

Under the free banking system, these state banks could issue bank notes against specie but the state regulated their interest rates and deposit rates, their reserve requirements and capital ratio. [8] The Michigan Act (1837) allowed the automatic chartering of banks that would fulfill its requirements without special consent of the state legislature. Accordingly, this legislation allowed the creation of unstable banks even further.

In 1797 there were only twenty-four chartered banks in the

United States. This figure ballooned to seven hundred and twelve in 1837. Needless to say, these banks were unstable and short-lived. The average life of a bank was five years. About fifty percent of these banks failed and approximately thirty-five percent could not redeem their notes.

[9] During the "Free Banking Era," the value of gold and silver was very stable. Price stability and change in price are two different things. When monetary bases (such as gold and silver) are allowed to stay relatively constant, that allows for all other prices to adjust quickly. If a price is quick to adjust (not sticky) it is said to be a stable price. Since most free banks were not backed by specie and, in order to offer some stability, several local banks essentially took over the functions of a central bank. Generally, conditions did not improve and the next era of banking came in 1863 and as with previous eras, the International Bankers were planning a scheme for a central bank through which they would control the United States monetary system.

1863-1913 – National Banks:

As with the War of 1812, the outbreak of the War Between the States required, in early 1863, a means of financing it. This led to a renewed interest in a central bank. [10] "With the lessons of the Second Bank, the designers took a different approach modeled of the Free Banking System." However, by the time this system had barely started, the National Banking Act of 1863 (which soon after was superseded by the Banking Act of 1864) came into being. The Act was federal law that established a system of national charters for banks and created the United States Banking System.

Under the Act, the office of Comptroller of the Currency was established to supervise these banks. The National Banks had much higher standards and better business practices than the state banks. Also under the Act, a national currency was created and required National Banks to accept each other's currency at par value. Bank notes (bills) were printed by the Comptroller to avoid counterfeiting. National Treasury securities enlarged the market and raised liquidity.

EARLY GAINS TOWARD WORLD CONTROL ►

Although National Banks quickly jumped to approximately fifteen hundred by 1865, there were still several hundred state banks in operation. The Federal Government imposed a ten percent tax on state banks and they slowly dwindled away.

While the foregoing was happening, what do you think the International Bankers were doing? You are correct if you thought they were vigorously working to gain control over the United States monetary system. By this time their power had grown extremely fast through ownership of banks and gaining control over several key banks and willing politicians.

The International Bankers were the real power in the creation of the National Banking Act. They assured certain factors were included that would lead to the downfall of the Act. With power of their banks and a great amount of influence over other banks, they were able to get the imposition of the ten percent tax upon state banks which put them out of business. Needless to say, they were like vultures waiting to swallow up the gap left by the demise of state banks, making their position even stronger. They had power and used it to make treasuries fluctuate in value causing instability in both national and state banks. With these fluctuations, banks had to recall loans or borrow from other banks. Liquidity demands became so strong that banks again had to find a lender of last resort which led to the Panic of 1907.

[11] J.P. Morgan, the Rothschild's most trusted and important investor of their interests in the United States, stepped in and saved the day during the Panic of 1907. In fact, he acted as an unofficial central bank for the United States economy.

Simultaneously with the foregoing, much maneuvering – both overtly and covertly – was transpiring toward the creation of a central bank. Naturally, the bank would be controlled by the International Bankers. Already controlling the wealth of Europe, the plan for world control of the monetary system, and eventually a One World Government, would be complete by the capture and control of the vast (present and future) wealth of the United States.

Several key players were working in various ways for the creation of a central bank. J.P. Morgan was using his huge amount of influence among prominent individuals, institutions, and politicians. Senator Nelson Aldrich of Rhode Island (Rothschild agent) personally ran the National Monetary Commission, leaning heavily upon a select group of economists. He traveled to Europe studying the German and British banking policies and procedures. In 1812, he presented his plan which never got off the ground as we will see in the next chapter. Nelson Aldrich persuaded Representative Carter Glass, Chairman of the House Committee on Banking and Currency, to support his (Aldrich's) plan. Later, Carter Glass was active in the creation of the Federal Reserve System. In early 1907, Paul Warburg, a Rothschild agent and partner of Kuhn Noeb and Company, published the first official reform plan which he called "A Plan for a Modern Central Bank." Also in early 1907, Jacob Schiff, chief executive officer of Kuhn Loeb and Company, while speaking to the New York Chamber of Commerce stated that "unless we have a central bank with adequate control of credit resources, the country is going to undergo the most severe and far-reaching money panic in its history." Naturally, both Paul Warburg and Jacob Schiff knew the Panic of 1907 was coming since both were prominent players in the planning of it.

Again, as promised in the preceding chapter, I will now discuss some of the individuals and two banks that were prominent during the period discussed. They are not in chronological order of importance:

[12] Kuhn Loeb and Company was founded by Abraham Kuhn and Solomon Loeb in 1867, creating a successful merchandise business in Cincinnati, Ohio. They then decided to move to New York and establish their bank. Company records show that when their partnership was established, they were able to capitalize it at five-hundred thousand dollars.

Approximately eight years later, Jacob Schiff (Rothschild trained) who was Solomon Loeb's son-in-law, joined the firm and began a remarkable reign as leader of the firm. Under Jacob Schiff's directorship, Kuhn Loeb and Company grew to be the most prestigious investment bank, second only to J.P. Morgan and Company. We can safely say Kuhn Loeb and Company was probably the most influential bank in the late nineteenth and early twentieth centuries.

After Jacob Schiff's death on September 25, 1920, the firm was successfully led by Otto Kahn and Felix Warburg. The firm's fortunes began to fade after World War II and lost its independence in 1977 when it merged with Lehman Brothers to create Lehman Brothers, Kuhn, Loeb, Inc.

[13] J.P. Morgan was born on April 14, 1837 and died on March 31, 1913. As creator of J.P. Morgan and Company, he probably was the most dominant American financier and broker of his time. He almost totally dominated corporate finance and industrial consolidation. For example, in 1892, he arranged the merger of Edison General Electric and Thomson-Houston Electric Company to form General Electric that continues to flourish. After financing the creation of the Federal Steel Company, he merged with the Carnegie Steel Company and several other companies to form the United States Steel Corporation.

As previously discussed, he singlehandedly saved the day during the Panic of 1907 by unofficially acting as a central for the United States economy. You can bet your bottom dollar that he was well rewarded. Most researchers and/or authors described him as making a big bundle during the period.

During the period of 1890-1913, J.P. Morgan was involved in almost any business of which one can think. Forty-two major corporations were organized or their securities were underwritten in whole or in part by J.P. Morgan and Company. Many are still in existence today and consist of fourteen industrial corporations and twenty-four railroads. For our purposes, at this point J.P. Morgan was the Rothschild's most trusted and important investor of their interests in the United States.

[14] Jacob Henry Schiff, born Jakob Heinrich Schiff (January 10, 1847 – September 25, 1920), was first employed in the banking and brokerage business in Frankfurt, Germany. After the War Between the States ended, Schiff came to the United States, settling in New York. He became a licensed broker and joined the firm of Budge, Schiff and

◄ ONCE THERE WAS AN AMERICA

Company in 1867. In 1872, he returned to Germany, but in 1874, Abraham Kuhn of Kuhn Loeb and Company invited him to return to New York and enter the firm.

Schiff accepted the invitation in January 1875, bringing his connections to some of the more prestigious banking firms in Europe. He married Teresa Loeb, daughter of Solomon Loeb on May 6, 1875. Ten years later he became head of Kuhn Loeb and Company and made it one of the most prominent banks in the United States. As we discussed earlier, he worked hard to establish a central bank in America.

[15] Paul Warburg was born in Hamburg, Germany. After his formal education, he became a protégé of the Rothschild who ensured his placement in the import and export business and banking positions in London and Paris.

The Rothschild had big future plans for Paul Warburg that would emerge in 1913. Paul Warburg was married to (who else?) Nina J. Loeb, daughter of Solomon Loeb, founder of Kuhn Loeb and Company. As we already know, he was an avid supporter of a central bank in America for which he was trained by the Rothschilds. We will see more of him in the next chapter.

CHAPTER 3

The Federal Reserve System

FROM CHAPTER TWO, we know that throughout the nineteenth century there was a poorly regulated banking system. Such a system resulted in many bank failures and financial panics. The Panic of 1907 was so severe that it created a huge clamor for a better system.

Starting with the Federal Reserve System, we will begin examining several of the many tentacles of the Evil Octopus's plan for a One World Government which was mostly hidden for two centuries. Today it is openly spoken of and supported by the most prominent figures and politicians of the United States whether knowingly or unknowingly.

I consider the Federal Reserve System as the number one and most dangerous of these evil tentacles. The others will be presented in no particular order. As we progress through the several tentacles, you must remember that they are entwined and interlocked although they may not appear to be. Certain groups may struggle for control while at the same time supporting their opposition on a particular issue or project. This is because the end result will essentially be the same: a one-world, two-class, non-religious, Socialist society.

We also know the American public had practically no trust in banks. Citizens of the Western and Southern states especially distrusted the more influential banks located in New York. On the other hand, most banks, led by the German-Jewish bankers, had nefarious plans to establish a central bank which, under their control, would give them access to the vast riches of the United States.

To assist in this scheme, certain politicians were under the thumb of the International Bankers and selected individuals in Europe were specifically trained in banking procedures to be helpful in formulating and implementing their plans. These individuals were later brought to the United States and placed in important banking firms and some married into New York banking families. [1] "At the time, intermarriage among the German-Jewish elite was customary. Consequently, the partners of Kuhn Loeb were closely related by blood and marriage to the partners of J&W Seligman, Speyer and Company, Goldman, Sachs and Company, and Lehman Brothers. A particularly close relationship existed between the partners of Kuhn, Loeb, and M.M. Warburg and Company of Hamburg, Germany, through Paul, Felix and Sigmund Warburg, who were Kuhn Loeb partners."

Probably every writer and/or researcher of the Federal Reserve System over the past fifty-five years gained much of their knowledge from [2] Eustace Mullins, author of the 1954 book "The Secrets of the Federal Reserve." I am no exception and I believe you should know a few facts about Mr. Mullins (October 30, 1923 – February 2, 2010). Mr. Mullins was educated at Washington and Lee University, New York University, the University of North Dakota, and the Institute of Contemporary Arts in Washington D.C. He worked for several newspapers and magazines and was the author of many books, articles, and pamphlets. In 1950, he was a researcher at the Library of Congress where he had access to a plethora of information which enabled him to write "Secrets of the Federal Reserve." Although still sought by many people, unfortunately the book is no longer in print. Shortly after his first book came out in 1952, he was discharged from the Library of Congress. Apparently he was getting too close to the truth.

Senator Nelson Aldrich of Rhode Island was reasonably influential in the United States Senate and, in 1910, was serving as Chairman of the National Monetary Commission. As a proponent of a central bank

THE FEDERAL RESERVE SYSTEM ➤

and under strong control of several International Bankers, Aldrich arranged a super secret meeting of a selected group of bankers or their representatives to be held in November of 1910 at the Jekyll Island Georgia Hunt Club. This meeting would later prove to be the greatest fraud ever perpetuated against the United States.

On the night of November 22, 1910, a railroad car with locks on the door and shades drawn was sitting at an infrequently used railroad track in Hoboken, New Jersey. Naturally, this railroad car and all expenses for this lengthy trip and meeting were arranged by Senator Aldrich at the expense of the United States Government.

Like lurking thieves, this group – consisting of Nelson W. Aldrich, his personal secretary Shelton, A. Piatt Andrews, Assistant Secretary of the Treasury, Henry P. Davison, senior partner of J.P. Morgan and Company, Charles D. Norton, President of the First National Bank of New York, Frank Vanderlip, President of the National City Bank of New York – snuck aboard the sealed railroad car. Prior to departure, the large group was joined by Benjamin Strong (another J.P. Morgan agent) and Paul Warburg, a member of Kuhn Loeb who had recently immigrated from Germany. Prior to leaving Germany, Paul Warburg was specifically trained for this meeting and, as we will see later, completely dominated it.

[3] Approximately six years later, Bertie Charles Forbes, who later founded *Forbes Magazine*: "Picture a party of the nation's greatest bankers stealing out of New York (actually New Jersey) on a private railroad car under the cover of darkness, stealthily hiding hundreds of miles south, embarking on a mysterious launch, sneaking onto an island deserted by all but a few servants, living there for a full week under such rigid secrecy that the names of not one of them was once mentioned lest the servants learn the identity and declare to the world this strangest, most secret expedition in the history of American finance." I am romanticizing; I am giving to the world, for the first time, the real story of how the famous Aldrich system was written.

The utmost secrecy was enjoined upon all. The public must not get a hint of what was to be done. Senator Aldrich notified each to go quietly into a private car which the railroad had received orders to draw upon an unfrequented platform. New York's ubiquitous reporters had been foiled. Nelson (Aldrich) had confided to Henry, Frank, Paul, and Platt that he was to keep them locked up Jekyll Island, out of the rest of the world, until they had evolved and completed a scientific currency system for the United States, the real birth of the present Federal Reserve System, the plan done on Jekyll Island in the conference with Paul, Frank, and Henry – Warburg is the link that binds the Aldrich system and the present system together. He, more than any one man, has made the system a working reality.

[4] The Aldrich group had no interest in hunting Jekyll Island, chosen for the site of the preparation of the central bank because it offered complete privacy, and because there was not a journalist within fifty miles. Such was the need for secrecy that the members of the party agreed, before arriving at Jekyll Island, that no last names would be used at any time during their two week stay. The group later referred to themselves as the "First Name Club," as the last names of Warburg, Strong, Vanderlip and others were prohibited during their stay. The customary attendants had been given a two-week vacation from the club and new servants were brought in from the mainland for this occasion who did not know the names of any of those present. Even if they had been interrogated after the Aldrich party went back to New York, they could not have given the names. This arrangement proved to be so satisfactory that the members later had a number of get-togethers in New York.

We may ask: why take such a long trip under utmost secrecy? Supposedly, the project was to write the banking and currency legislation which the National Monetary Commission had ordered to be prepared in public. [5] At stake was the future control of the money and credit of the United States. If any genuine monetary reform had been prepared and presented to Congress, it would have ended the power of the elitist, one-world, money creation. Jekyll Island ensured that a central bank would be established in the United States which would give these banks everything they had always wanted.

THE FEDERAL RESERVE SYSTEM

As previously planned and because of his banking knowledge and special training, Paul Warburg was responsible for practically all of the drafting of the plan. Warburg's drafts would be discussed by the group and when appropriate, changes were made. This was especially true of Senator Aldrich since he had political knowledge of what form of completed plan could get by Congress. All members of the party played their roles according to their expertise because there could be no mistakes. Once they left Jekyll Island, it would be impossible to have others secret meetings in order to change the plan.

Despite a strenuous and productive nine-day period, the project did not go without some turmoil and personality clashes. Senator Aldrich considered himself as the leader and in accordance with his personality, tried to order everyone else around, even though he was the only non-banker in the group. Paul Warburg's natural German-Jewish pushy, arrogant personality and his alien accent grated on everyone. Warburg took every opportunity to give a detailed talk aimed to impress the group of his banking experience. He contested group members on every occasion concerning technical banking questions and constantly reminded the group that they had to accept his presence if a central bank was to be devised which would guarantee them their future profits.

Henry P. Davison was deliberately placed in the Aldrich Group by J.P. Morgan because of his diplomacy in defusing heated discussions. Accordingly, Davison kept the discord down to a minimum and can be considered the catalyst that kept them working. However, it did not take long (almost from the beginning) for it to become apparent that Paul Warburg was the real power and would be the architect of the plan. No one dared to contest this fact since they all knew he was Rothschild's appointed man for the task at hand.

From the onset, Paul Warburg stressed to the group that the main problem was to avoid the name "Central Bank." Instead he selected the name "Federal Reserve" to deceive the American public into thinking it was not a central bank plan. Regardless of this deception, Warburg's plan would be a central bank plan that fulfilled the main functions of a Central Bank; it would be owned by private individuals who would profit from the ownership of shares. As a bank of issue, it would control the United States money and credit.

There was great deal of heated discussion that the Reserve Bank was to be controlled by Congress and answerable to the government. However, the majority of the board of directors was to be chosen by the banks of the association. Again, Paul Warburg stepped in and refined the plan whereby the Federal Reserve Board of Governors would be appointed by the President of the United States. Thus, the "real" work of the Board would be controlled by the Federal Reserve Advisory Council, meeting with the Governors. This Council would be chosen by the directors of the twelve Federal Banks (more on this later) and the Council members would remain unknown to the President of the United States.

We already know from earlier discussion that most American citizens detest the New York Wall Street Bankers and their political representatives would never vote for any plan that smelled of New York. This was especially true of the bankers in the West and South who detested the underhanded practices of the New York bankers. To conceal this fact, Paul Warburg devised a scheme which would prevent the citizens from recognizing his plan as a central bank. Warburg's scheme was a proposal to set up a regional reserve system. Twelve branches of reserve banks would be located in different sections of the country. Therefore, very few people outside the banking industry would realize that the existing concentration of the nation's money and credit structure in New York made the proposal of regional reserve system a delusion.

Paul Warburg insisted that the administrators of the twelve branch reserve banks that be appointed by the President of the United States. This would remove the system from Congressional control. This was absolutely unconstitutional since the Federal Reserve System was to be a bank of issue and Article One, Section Eight of the United States Constitution specifically charges Congress with "the power to coin money and regulate the value thereof."

THE FEDERAL RESERVE SYSTEM

As was the mindset of all International Banks (Evil Octopus), they had no respect for the Constitution. It was a fact and belief among these banks that "who controls the money of a country also controls the country." They knew that the approval of the Federal Reserve System would also give them control of the President (then and now) and the Judicial Branch was already controlled by the President through presidential appointment. Furthermore, they already had a plan of bypassing Congress.

As we now know, the Jekyll Island plan was a fraud from the beginning. Nevertheless, the plan was presented to Congress as the completed work of the National Monetary System and the time spent at Jekyll Island on this plan was not known for some time.

[6] Shortly after their return to New York, the Jekyll Island conspirators began a national propaganda campaign to persuade the American public that the so-called Aldrich plan should be enacted into law by Congress. The International Bankers had set up a five million dollar (a lot of money from 1931-1932) slush fund to finance this propaganda machine. Three of America's leading universities – Harvard, Princeton, and the University of Chicago – were selected to oversee this national propaganda program.

It was frequently stated by numerous politicians, businessmen, and bankers that Professor J. Lawrence Laughlin of the University of Chicago did more than any one man in getting Senator Nelson Aldrich's bill approved by Congress. For example, Congressman Charles A. Lindbergh, Sr. stated, "J. Lawrence Laughlin, Chairman of the Executive Committee of the National Citizens League since its organization, has returned to his position as professor of political economics in the University of Chicago." In June 1911, Professor Laughlin was given a year's leave from the university that he might give all of his time to the campaign of education understanding by the League – "He has worked indefatigigably, and it is largely due to his efforts and his per sentence that the campaign enters the final stage with flattering prospects of a successful outcome ... The reader knows that the University of Chicago is an institution endowed by John D.

Rockefeller, with nearly fifty million dollars."

The Wall Street/International Bankers already knew the influence that the news media had over the American public and in future years would finance individuals and corporations of their ilk in owning practically all of the mass media which is one-sided and very Anti-American and Socialist-leaning. The National Citizens League spent almost all of the five million dollar slush fund, using all known media to include writing and distributing pamphlets, sponsoring rallies, radio programs, newspaper ads, and in or two instances even outright buying newspapers. The control of the entire wealth and credit of the United States was at stake and, to the conspirators, anything ethical or unethical was fair game.

In 1910, communication of information was slow, with most official information distributed by the postal system. If a meeting to discuss aspects of the Aldrich Bill was to be held on a specific date and in a specific city, the Aldrich operatives would deliberately hold back on mailing the information so that opposition would receive it at the last moment and often would not have enough time to read the contents and be prepared for the scheduled meeting. An example of such tactics follows:

When Andrew Frame testified before the House of Banking and Currency Committee of the American Banking Association, he was representing a group of Western bankers who opposed the Aldrich Plan. Part of the testimony proceeded as follows:

[7] Chairman Carter Glass: "Why didn't the Western bankers make themselves heard when the American Bankers Association gave its unqualified answer, we are assured, unanimous approval of the scheme proposed by the National Monetary Commission?"

Andrew Frame: "I'm glad you called my attention to that. When that monetary bill was given to the country, it was but a few days previous to the meeting of the American Bankers Association in New Orleans in 1911. There was not one banker in a hundred who had read that bill. We had twenty addresses in favor of it. General Hamby of Austin, Texas wrote a letter to President Watts asking for a hearing against the bill. He did not get a very courteous answer. I refused to vote on it, and a great many others did likewise."

Mr. Buckley: "Do you mean that no member of the Association could be heard in opposition to the bill?"

Andrew Frame: "They throttled all argument."

Mr. Kindred: "But the report was given out that it was lased unanimous."

Andrew Frame: "The bill had already been prepared by Senator Aldrich and presented to the executive council of the American Bankers Association in May 1911. As a member of the Council, I received a copy the day before they acted upon it. When the bill came in at New Orleans, the bankers of the United States had not read it."

Mr. Kindred: "Did the presiding officer simply rule out those wanted to discuss it negatively?"

Andrew Frame: "They would not allow anyone on the program who was not in favor of the bill."

Chairman Glass: "What significance has the fact that at the next annual meeting of the American Bankers Association held at Detroit in 1912, the Association did not reiterate its endorsement of the plan of the National Monetary Commission, known as the Aldrich scheme?"

Andrew Frame: "It did not reiterate the endorsement for the simple fact that the backers of the Aldrich Plan knew that the Association would not endorse it. We were ready for them, but they did not bring it up."

You will recall that years earlier Senator Aldrich had coaxed Representative Carter Glass into supporting a central bank system, but now they were taking different approaches in many committee meetings, debates, etc. throughout the period of 1911-1912. As a point of clarification, you should remember that terms such as the Aldrich Plan, The Plan, and the Federal Reserve Act are synonymous.

[8] "The Federal Reserve Act spent most of 1913 being debated in Congress and in public." Many additional powers came out in support of the Act including Socialist-leaning Woodrow Wilson. Wilson was guided by Marxist "handler" Edward Mendell House, an agent of

the International Bankers.

The Federal Reserve Act was very narrowly passed by Congress in November 1913. It was signed by President Woodrow Wilson and enacted December 31, 1913 creating the Federal Reserve System, the central banking system of the United States. And granted it the legal authority to issue legal tender.

The following are some additional points to ponder:

1. [9] The Federal Reserve System is absolutely unconstitutional. Congress could not legally give up "the power to coin and print currency and regulate the value thereof."
2. [10] "The seven members of the Board of Governors are appointed by the President and confirmed by the Senate to serve a fourteen-year term in office. Members may serve only one full term. The President designates and the Senate confirms two members of the Board to be Chairman and Vice Chairman for four-year terms." This process is per functionary since the President and the Senate do not oppose the Fed.
3. [11] "The primary responsibility of the Board members is the formation of monetary policy. The seven board members constitute a majority of the twelve-member Federal Open Market Commission, the group that makes the key decisions affecting the cost and availability of money and credit in the economy. The other five members of FOMC are Reserve Bank Presidents, one of whom is the president of the Federal Reserve Bank of New York. The other Bank Presidents serve one-year terms on a rotating basis. By statute, the FOMC determines its own organization, and by tradition, it elects the Chairman and the President of the New York Bank as its Vice Chairman." There are many more functions of the board but I will not present them. By now, you should realize that the Federal Reserve System is not Federal at all and the United States Government has no control over it.
4. All the audits of the Federal Reserve System are conducted [12]

THE FEDERAL RESERVE SYSTEM

either internally or by private outside auditing firms. Unless there has been a recent change the GAO lacks audit authority over the Federal Reserve's monetary policy, foreign transactions, and Open Market Committee operations.

5. [13] The Federal Reserve System operates independent of the President, the rest of the Executive Branch, and the Legislation Branch. The Federal Reserve gets its authority from Congress and its subject (Ha! Ha!) to congressional oversight.

The Federal Reserve is a federal as Federal Express. It is not part of or regulated by the United States Government. Since you cannot compete in banking without being part of this money trust cartel, it also has the ability to control interest rates and other banking requirements like what fraction of loans must be held in reserve as part of the fractional banking scheme.

6. [14] Global Research sums up a lengthy article as follows: (1) The Fed is privately owned. Its shareholders are private banks. In fact, one hundred percent of its shareholders are private banks. None of its stock is owned by the United States Government. (2) The fact that the Fed does not get "appropriations" from Congress basically means that it gets its money from Congress without Congressional approval by engaging in "open market operations."
7. The Fed generates profit for its shareholders.
8. [15] "In 1913 Congress delegated the power to the Fed to coin money and regulate the value thereof and can reclaim it at any time." I am ready to push Congress to do so. Are you?

There is so much more to be written about the Federal Reserve System, but I will end our discussion with one more item. We already know that the Chairman of the Board of Governors of the Federal Reserve System is appointed by the President for four-year periods. I have researched all Chairmen and, with the exception of Charles

◄ ONCE THERE WAS AN AMERICA

S. Hamlin, all have connections of some type to the International Bankers (The Evil Octopus).

CHAIRMAN	FROM	TO	PRESIDENT(S)
Charles S. Hamlin	8/10/14	8/19/16	Woodrow Wilson
William G. Harbin	8/10/16	8/19/22	Woodrow Wilson
Daniel R. Crossing	5/11/23	9/15/27	Warren G. Harding
Roy A. Young	10/4/27	8/31/30	Calvin Coolidge
Eugene Meyer	9/10/30	5/10/33	Herbert Hoover
Eugene R. Black	5/19/33	8/15/34	Franklin D. Roosevelt
Marvin S. Eccles	11/15/34	1/31/48	Franklin D. Roosevelt Franklin D. Roosevelt
Thomas B. McCabe	4/1/48	3/31/51	Harry S. Truman
William McChesney Martin	4/2/51	1/31/70	Harry S. Truman
Arthur F. Burns	1/11/70	1/31/78	Harry S. Truman Dwight D. Eisenhower John F. Kennedy Richard M. Nixon Richard M. Nixon Gerald Ford Jimmy Carter
G. William Miller	3/8/78	8/6/79	Jimmy Carter
Paul A. Volcker	8/6/70	8/11/87	Jimmy Carter Ronald W. Reagan
Alan Greenspan	8/1/87	1/31/2006	Ronald W. Reagan George H.W. Bush Bill Clinton George W. Bush
Ben Bernake	2/11/2006	–	George W. Bush Barrack Obama

◄ 34

CHAPTER **4**

Immigration And Labor Unions

CHAPTER ONE, I pointed out that the Evil Octopus (Illuminati/ International Bankers) had many tentacles. With the passage of time, more and more tentacles have emerged and today there are actually hundreds of them in varying types and degrees of importance. In Chapter Three, we discussed the Federal Reserve System in great depth because it was/is the first and most dangerous of the tentacles.

IMMIGRATION:

With the exception of American Indians, all of us are immigrants or descendents of immigrants. I take the risk of saying probably less than five percent of our national population knows the influence immigration has had on the United States society. We will take a look at the impact on several areas of our society such as labor, politics, economics, and social unrest.

In the study of immigration, it is nearly impossible to completely separate immigration from the earlier labor movement in the United States. This is due to their interlocking in politics, labor and other areas of society. I will try to keep them separated to the best of my ability since we will be going further into labor unions later in this chapter.

Immigrants have been coming to American since our first colony was founded in Virginia with the door wide open. George Washington asserted that [1] "the bosom of America is open to receive not only the opulent and respected stronger, but the oppressed and persecuted of all nations and religions, which we share welcome to a participation of all our rights and privileges." The view of George Washington lasted for a time, but it was not very long until turmoil began to emerge. Consequently, various acts and laws were implemented to control such turmoil.

We will initially look at [2] three periods of massive numbers of immigration to the United States. We will also look at more recent periods that have had a pronounced effect on our society. Immigrants came to America for various reasons such as escape from religious persecution, political turmoil, criminal activity, etc. By far, most came for economic reasons. In due course, they became a part of migratory systems that responded to changing demands in labor markets. In looking at these periods, keep in mind (1) we are speaking of European immigration since Chinese and Japanese immigrants were not yet allowed, (2) economic conditions throughout the 1800s in Europe were in turmoil, (3) the United States economy had a huge need for both skilled and unskilled workers prior to 1800, and (4) after 1800, practically all of our need was for unskilled workers for the growing demand in factory jobs.

THREE PERIODS OF MASSIVE IMMIGRATION:
1. 1815-1860 – Five million immigrants settled permanently in the United States, mainly English, Irish, German, Scandinavian, and others from Northwestern Europe.
2. 1865-1890 – Ten million immigrants settled permanently in the United States, again mainly from Northwestern Europe.
3. 1890-1914 – Fifteen million immigrants came to the United States, many (some will say mostly) whom were Austro-Hungarian, Turkish, Lithuanian, Russian, and Jewish.

Although the overwhelming majority of immigrants from the periods listed above came for factory of other lower-paying jobs, there

IMMIGRATION AND LABOR UNIONS

was always a group of professionals. This element consisted of university professors, economists, philosophers, engineers, etc. Many of these professionals had been previously sought out and sponsored by influential persons or groups in the United States. This was especially true of university professors who had a Socialist background. They were placed in well-known colleges and universities and, as was the plan, many became university presidents and the "chosen" students were prepared for the same and years later replaced their retiring mentors. Other educators were placed in other colleges and universities predominately in the Northeast. This was the beginning of the rapid rise in Socialist influence and later, control of the United States education system which we will discuss later.

The professionals were not alone in the sponsoring of selected individuals. The labor movement sought out those who knew how to organize, effectively lead group demonstrations, and even Anarchists who were used to promote unrest, coordinate organizers and local group leaders. They were also used to promote violence when deemed necessary.

During the late 1880s and throughout the 1890s, there was a huge amount of turmoil in the labor movement and a great deal of unrest in political and social matters. Much of this turmoil can be attributed to most immigrants settling in the larger cities of that period which consisted of New York, Boston, Pittsburgh, and Chicago. The various ethnic groups settled into their own areas of the cities and often bordered each other. Living conditions in practically all areas were very undesirable, overcrowded, and unsanitary.

As a result of social and economic unrest, the so-called "Native Americans" (immigrants prior to 1800) became restless and blamed most of the unrest on those immigrants from Southwestern Europe who came after 1890. These immigrants were considered "inferior" to all who migrated prior to 1890. [3] "By 1910, Eastern and Southern Europeans made up seventy percent of the immigrants entering the United States." After 1914, immigration rapidly dropped off because of World War I.

◄ ONCE THERE WAS AN AMERICA

Among the many incidents of turmoil and the most significant, was the Haymarket Affair, also known as the [4] Haymarket Massacre or Haymarket Riot. This incident took place at the Haymarket Square in Chicago on May 4, 1886. It started as a rally in support of striking workers, but suddenly an unknown person threw a dynamite bomb at the Chicago police as they were in the process of dispensing the meeting. The blast and the ensuing gunfire resulted in the death of eight police officers from an unknown number of civilians. Later, in legal proceedings eight Anarchists were tried for murder and executed. One committed suicide in prison, although the prosecution admitted none of the defendants had thrown the bomb.

Although May Day celebrations, in many forms, have been around for several hundred years, the Haymarket Affair is generally considered significant for the origin of international May Day observance for union workers.

The Haymarket Affair was the incident that pushed Native Americans to a critical point where government action had to be taken against the prevailing turmoil. Several influential organizations, such as the Immigration Restriction League, were formed to pressure Congress for reformation. [5] In 1907, the United States Senate, under pressure from these groups, formed the Dillingham Commission to study the origin and consequences of immigration. In a series of reports published in 1910 and 1911, the Commission claimed the crucial shift in European immigration patterns corresponded with the rise of festering social and economic problems in the United States.

[6] The Emergency Quota Act, also known as the Emergency Immigration Act of 1921, the Immigration Restriction Act of 1921, the Per Centum Law, and the Johnson Quota Act, restricted immigrants to the United States. Despite the fact that it was intended as temporary legislation, it proved to be the most important turning point in American immigration policy since it added two new features to the immigration law: numerical limits on immigration from Europe and the use of a quota system for establishing those limits.

Under this act, immigrants from any country were restricted to

IMMIGRATION AND LABOR UNIONS

three percent (annually) to the number to residents from that same country living in the United States as of the U.S. Census of 1910. The use of such a National Origins Formula continued until 1965. As in the past, this allowed a large influx of Socialist educators who were strategically placed in our education system. Additionally, this act set no limits on immigrants from Latin America.

From 1921 to the present time of 2011, there have been numerous immigration acts, amendments to acts, and various laws pertaining to immigration. Although all are informative, I will only cover three more and will not go into extensive detail.

[7] The Immigration Act of 1924, also known as the Johnson Reed Act, replaced the Emergency Quota Act which had been in effect only three years. This act, as with the Emergency Quota Act, came about as a result of intensive public pressure that included the well-known union leader and founder of the American Federation of Labor, Samuel Rompers.

Under the provisions of this act, it limited the number of immigrants who could be admitted from any country to two percent of the number of people from that country who were already living in the United States in 1890, down from three percent set by the Emergency Quota Act of 1921. This act governed American immigration policy until 1952.

[8] The Immigration and Nationality Act of 192 governs primarily immigration and citizenship. From December 24, 1952 to the present, the definition of the "United States" for national purposes expanded to include Guam, the Commonwealth of Northern Mariana Islands, Puerto Rico, and the United States Virgin Islands. Persons born in these territories on or prior to December 24, 1952 acquire citizenship at birth.

Previous radical restrictions were abolished, but a quota system was retained and the policy of restricting the number of immigrants from certain countries continued. The act defined the type of immigrants, allowed for the deportation of immigrants or naturalized engaged in subversive activities, and allowed the barring of suspected subversives from entering the country. It was used over the years to bar members and former members and "fellow travelers" of the Communist Party. The act also allowed for the system where either group were desirable immigrants and placed great importance on labor qualifications. The act had been used to exclude numerous prominent individuals until its ideological clauses were repealed in 1990. It is interesting to note that among this large group was Pierre Trudeau, prior to his becoming Prime Minister of Canada.

[9] The Immigration and Nationality Act of 1965, also known as the Hart-Cellar Act, dramatically changed the method by which immigrants were admitted to the United States. This act not only allowed more individuals from third-world countries to enter the United States, including Asia, who had previously been hindered from entering America, but it also allowed a special quota for refugees. Under the act, one hundred and seventy thousand immigrants from the Eastern Hemisphere were granted residency, with no more than twenty thousand per country. One hundred and twenty thousand immigrants from the Western Hemisphere with no nationality restrictions were also admitted. As usual, a provision was made that future immigrants were to be welcomed because of their professional skills.

[10] Although Lyndon B. Johnson signed the bill, John F. Kennedy was pushing for this act prior to his death. After his death, his brother Robert Kennedy – United States Attorney General and Senator Ted Kennedy vigorously pushed the act which later became official. We can safely say that by approving this act, the United States flung open its door to the world.

To those who have taken the time to study, we find that as the government grew more liberal, politicians became less informed and less patriotic, combined with the citizens becoming more hedonistic and the United States immigration policy is in complete chaos. Personally, I see it as planned, through creeping (Fabian) Socialism. You will note that in each act we have covered, there was always a means whereby certain selected individuals were automatically admitted. This is especially true for academics, philosophy, and economics. Also, if you will take the time to think and do a small bit of research, you will find that neither of our two major political nor presidents have done anything to correct this immigration mess. I am sure much of this is because of the fear of losing minority votes (they take the rest of us for granted) and under the current administration there is a desire and plan to reduce the United States to a second- or third-world level.

To practically all of our politicians, the preference and desire of the American public does not seem to matter. To emphasize the foregoing, I present two examples:

1. [11] In a Zogby American Poll taken April 17-24, 2006, seventy-three percent of American citizens had little to no confidence in the United States Government to weed out terrorists or criminals if an amnesty program is instituted.

2. [12] A Fox News/Opinion Dynamics Poll taken April 4-5, 2006 of nine hundred registered voters showed the following:
   » 90% think that illegal immigration is a very serious problem.
   » 87% think that illegal immigrants will overburden government programs.
   » 81% think that it is unfair to grant rights to illegal immigrants while thousands wait to come to the United States illegally.
   » 75% are concerned that illegal immigration will lead to an increase in crime.
   » 73% favor imposing fines and criminal charges against employers who hire illegal immigrants.
   » 74% said that the United States is not doing enough to keep illegal immigrants from crossing over into the United States.
   » 74% said that they favor providing major penalties for employers convicted of hiring illegal immigrants and strongly enforcing it.

» 50% said that they favor deporting all illegal immigrants back to their country; 45% said that they "oppose;" 49% did not know. When asked if they would favor allowing illegal immigrants already working in the United States to register as guest workers for a fixed periods of time so that the government could keep track of them, 73% said that they favor this, 23% said that they oppose, and 3% did not know.
» 71% are convinced that illegal immigrants increase crime.
» 56% think that illegal immigrants are taking the jobs that citizens do not want.

Similar and up-to-date polls closely compare to the above polls taken in 2006. Recently and with disgust for the lack of concern of the Obama administration, certain states have begun to institute laws to correct the failure of the Federal Government. During the month of May 2011, the Supreme Court of Georgia approved a law similar to that of Arizona.

In closing out this discussion, it appears that our current United States Government and the Obama administration have no concern for our immigration laws. Accordingly, state governments are beginning to carry the load of an incompetent regime in Washington D.C. It is interesting to note that citizens have come out of their state of lethargy on this issue and are supporting state officials.

LABOR UNIONS:

From the way I present the facts on the subject of labor unions, you may think I am Anti-Union. Please be assured that I am not. I simply present the information in a truthful manner, learned from firsthand experience, formal education, and personal research. Labor Relations was the area of concentration in my Master of Public Administration Degree program and I have been a union member of the International Brotherhood of Electrical Workers Union, served as a Union Steward of a small local and have helped negotiate contracts on the union's side of the table and on the side of management. I have also served as a Labor Relations Coordinator (for management) with two Federal Employee Unions.

Academicians have taught students and written books throughout many decades that there was and/or are very little Communist/Socialist influence in the United States Labor Unions. This is absolutely false. However, it is true that the rise of labor unions did not produce a large number of members into either the Socialist Party or the Communist Party as expected. Regardless of this fact, union leaders have accepted the philosophy of these subversive parties and have practiced it from the early days of movement until the present. Union leaders have been very astute of, and successful in, utilizing the tactics learned from the Communist and Socialist Parties.

When we think of certain circumstances in today's study of labor unions, many people ask the questions: "Are labor unions necessary?" They may quote how the extremely high wages of workers and huge retirement packages of the United Auto Workers Union forced the automobile industry into a non-competitive position and taxpayer money was necessary to bail them out to avoid a shutdown of the industry. At the same time, they will point to Toyota's success in right-to-work states where workers did not have to join a union, thus employment remained high and wages were very satisfactory to workers.

Our colleges and universities may claim that they science of management has reached a level where managers are trained to treat workers in such a humane manner that unions are unnecessary. They refer to the fact that graduates in management programs at both the baccalaureate and master degree levels have studied in such areas as human relations, organizational behavior, etc. and will manage in such a humane manner that the need for organized labor is no longer needed.

The foregoing premises are far from the truth. Many years ago when logic was taught in our educational system (and should still be taught), we were taught that the human being, in essence, is evil.

◄ **ONCE THERE WAS AN AMERICA**

We must remember that management function is to make the highest margin of profit for the owner or shareholder. Managers at all levels of the organization are judged (and paid) by how well they contribute to the profit margin. Without a union or the threat of a union, it would not take long for the organization to revert to a form of management practiced more than a century ago. To better understand both sides of the topic, we should look at early management practices, labor tactics, outside influences, and a few labor laws.

[13] The Sherman Anti-Trust Act of 1890 was not a true labor law but played a role in one of the better known labor cases several years later. This act authorized the Federal Government to bring proceedings against trusts in order to dissolve them. Unfortunately, a Supreme Court ruling prevented federal authorities from using the act for several years. Due to President Theodore Roosevelt's "trust busting" campaign, the Sherman Anti-Trust Act began to be invoked and, in 1904, the Supreme Court upheld the government in its suit for dissolution of the Northern Securities Company. After this case, the act was used more often with a high rate of success. Many of you will remember that the act broke up the American Telephone and Telegraph monopoly in 1982.

[14] The National Labor Relations Act is a 1935 United States Federal Law that limits the means by which employers may react to workers in the private sector who create labor unions, engage in collective bargaining, and take part in strikes and other forms of concentrated activity in support of their demands. The act does not apply to workers in several other categories.

The National Labor Relations Act defined and prohibited five unfair labor practices. These provisions still exist, while others have been added under later legislation. The original employers' unfair labor practices consisted of:

1. Interfering with, restraining, and coercing employees in their rights under Section Seven. These rights include: freedom of association, mutual aid of protection, self-organization, the

IMMIGRATION AND LABOR UNIONS

   right to form, join, or assist labor organizations, to bargain collectively for wages and working conditions through representatives of their own choosing, and to engage in other protected, concentrated activities with or without a union.
2. Dominating or interfering with the formation of any labor organization.
3. Discriminating against employees to discourage acts of support for a labor organization.
4. Discrimination against employees who files charges or testify.
5. Refusing to bargain collectively with the representative of the employees.

Prior to the enactment of labor laws, most employers treated their workers in a shockingly cruel manner. In many factories, workers in the Northern United States were treated worse than slaves in the South. The employees were forced to work in buildings that were unsanitary, unventilated, unheated, and, in general, unfit for human habitation. No safety precautions were taken to prevent injury from dangerous machinery, materials, or chemicals.

It was not unusual for workers to be forced to work extremely long hours, up to sixteen hours per days, six days per week. Wages were pitifully low and child labor as used in a similar manner. It was also not unusual for children as young as nine or ten years of age to work full, adult schedules. Although I could not find them for this book, I have seen authentic photographs of children being chained to the machinery on which they were working. Management's explanation of this practice was that it was necessary to keep them from wandering off and getting hurt.

I will present two significant and famous cases that show working conditions in the early twentieth century. There are many other labor related cases but these were cases that I had to study and write reports on during one of my courses related to labor relations. Fortunately, I kept some of my notes (though many years old) that allowed me to easily refresh my memory and locate reference material.

[15] The Danbury Hatters case of 1908 was the first United States Supreme Court case to find that the Sherman Anti-Trust Act applied to organized labor. Union leaders sought relief for many years. The Clayton Act of 1914 seemed to offer such relief. However, its labor provisions were ambiguous and unions did not win exemption from anti-trust litigation until the late 1930s.

The case stemmed from the efforts of the United Hatters of North America to unionize a hat company in Danbury, Connecticut. Although most hat companies had become unionized, Dietrich Lowe refused to unionize, preferring to undersell competition by paying sub-standard wages and failing to improve hazardous working conditions. The union responded with a strike and boycott, with the boycott backed by the American Federation of Labor.

Although most writers of this case put emphasis on the sub-standard wages, there were [16] dozens of cases of severe mercurialis found among workers. To understand how these cases came about, we will need to take a look at the process of making felt hats.

As a prelude, we must realize that Dietrich Lowe's plant did not offer any form of air circulation or ventilation nor did he provide any protection against mercury fumes, such as masks or other protective gear.

To make felt, hatters (workers) separate fur from the skin of small animals in a process known as carrotting. In this process, the secondary nitrous gas released from mercury nitrate caused the fur to turn orange, lose shape, and shrink. The fur then becomes darker, coiled, and more easily removed. And yes, throughout this process the hatters are breathing in the dangerous fumes. It was not until December 1,1941 that the United States Public Health Service brought an end to mercury use by hat makers in twenty-six states through mutual agreement.

The immigration population grew to record heights in the 1910s and, as the United States grew, so did the labor unions. Unfair working conditions continued despite union gains. Several laws were passed but most factory or shop owners deliberately failed to enforce

IMMIGRATION AND LABOR UNIONS ➤

most of the provisions of such laws. The "sweat shops" of the garment industry in New York City were notorious in unfair working conditions and produced, to my knowledge, the most tragic incident in the United States Labor Movement.

[17] On March 25, 1911, the worst factory fire in United States history took place in New York City. The owners of the Triangle Shirtwaist Factory ignored safety regulations. The laws stipulated that doors were to open outward. Triangle's doors opened inward. The company violated many other laws, such as keeping doors locked in order to keep track of their employees. When the fire broke out, the young women and girls had no place to go except to jump from the factory windows. One hundred and forty-six young women and girls died as a result of Triangle's breaking of safety laws.

The devastation of the fire brought much-needed attention to the working conditions in factories. New York adopted new laws and penalties for business owners who would not abide by the regulations. Naturally, the American Federation of Labor and other union organizations continued to push for improvements for the American worker.

The last topic I will present on the "bad" side of business owners is that of strike-breakers. Many companies, when faced with attempts of their business to become unionized took every action they could think of to prevent union presence in their companies and strike-breakers were the most dramatic.

Due to the long and violent nature of the labor movement, strike-breaker agencies were organized and readily available to company owners. One individual in New York City, known as the "king of strike-breakers," boasted of his roster of thirty-five thousand strike-breakers, and that he could muster several thousands of strike-breakers within the matter of an hour.

Strike-breakers consisted of thugs, ex-prize fighters, ex-murderers/convicts, and, in essence, criminals and hoodlums of every type. Their weapons consisted of baseball bats, blackjacks, knives, pistols, rifles, and on certain occasions, even dynamite and fire.

ONCE THERE WAS AN AMERICA

The history of the United States Labor Movement is replete with violent, bloody clashes between the strike-breakers and union members, and union organizations, members, picket line crossers, and then union's own brand of thugs. Consequently, the unions were not without fault, as we shall soon see.

Unions were well-funded through various individuals and organizations that used their own funds and served as conduits for funds coming from the International Bankers (The Evil Octopus) or their agents. Most of these agents were Communists, Socialists, and radicals of various stripes. From our study of immigration, you will recall that Anarchists, union organizers (thugs), Socialist educators, etc. were assisted in immigrating to the United States and funds for this program were furnished by the International Bankers. You may ask: "Why is this so?" It is simple when you seriously think about it. The International Bankers were making a bundle from the rapid rise of industry in America and they could control the industry from both ends, i.e. ownership and labor. A few bloody riots and a few hundred dead Americans did not bother them at all. Such activities diverted public attention from other objectives that had in mind. For example, they wanted and eventually gained control of the United States Education system, as we will see later.

With an abundance of money, union organizers were easily able to supplement the rabble brought from Europe. They hired, as permanent employees, the same type of characters who worked for strike-breakers. These "employees" were given jobs that required little physical effort, such as door guards, night watchers, and fire watchers. They were trained to respond to any attempt by management to dilute union power and influence, to recruit and brainwash new union members, and to arouse and lead union members when a strike was imminent. Some of the Pacifist/Socialist/Communist supporters of union organization and activities were:

1. The Fellowship of Reconciliation was founded in the United States in 1915. Although considered a Pacifist organization,

among its members was Norman Tomas who ran for President of the United States on the Socialist Ticket.
2. Communist Brookwood Labor College. More on this later.
3. The committee on Militarism in Education.
4. A.J. Must. More on him later.
5. American Workers Party (1821-1929) – direct antecedent of the Communist Party, U.S.A.
6. Communist International Workers of the World.
7. Civil Liberties Bureau – forerunner of the American Civil Liberties Union, a Marxist organization led by Roger Baldwin. There will be much more on the American Liberties Union in a later chapter.
8. Jane Addams – political activist who defended many Anarchists and co-founder with her long-term lesbian lover, Ellen Gates Starr, of the Hull House in Chicago.
9. Elizabeth Gurley Flynn – became Chairman of the Communist Party, U.S.A.
10. Many others of the same ilk include Max Eastman, Walter Nelles, Scott Nearing, and Rabbi Stephen Wise.

[18] "There have always been radical parties and organizations in the labor movement whose self-proclaimed goal was not just improvement of the working conditions, but the creation of a different kind of society. They include Communists, Socialists, Trotsskysists, Musteites, Social Labor and several others." Before we leave this subject, we will take a closer look at some of these individuals and organizations, although we have already covered Communism and Socialism in unions to a large extent.

The Communist Party United State of America (CAUSA), for all practical purposes, dominated the labor movement from 1919-1937. However, [19] "The Profintern, or Red International of labor forced the Communist Party to change in 1921 when it directed United States Communists to work within the American Federation of Labor in order to make it a revolutionary body. This process was referred to as "boring from within." In order to accomplish this, the Profintern recognized the Trade Union Educational League, an organization founded by William Z. Foster, as its United States Affiliate.

[20] William Z. Foster established the Trade Union Educational League in 1920. The organization was subsidized by the Communist International from 1922 until 1928. After 1928, the organization was transferred into the Trade Union Unity League. Prior to this transfer, members did not pay dues but sought to both fund itself and spread its ideas through the sale of pamphlets and the circulation of a monthly magazine. Naturally, they received donations from various sources, again serving as conduits for the International Bankers. We could discuss many more aspects of Communists in the United States Labor Movement during the period of 1919-1937, but we will look at only two more cases and others that are more modern than these periods.

[21] Between 1918 and 1921, a number of unions, thinkers, and educators within the American Labor Movement founded a wide variety of adult education and training organizations. Among the many different types of organizations created were labor colleges. They were experiments of higher education designed to meet the needs of the labor movement as well as the educational needs of its often uneducated adult members.

Despite unions being adequately funded by the International Bankers, Brookwood College was also founded by a number of Socialist and Pacifist labor activists. For example, William Mann Fincke, a liberal clergyman and son of a mine owner, donated his family's fifty-three acre estate which included a large colonial farmhouse. Evelyn Preston, a wealthy liberal philanthropist donated fifty thousand dollars to build a new women's dormitory. Josephine and Martin Toscan Bennett donated their Katonah, New York property. The Garland Fund contributed heavily and, to understand its significance, we will need to discuss it separately.

[22] For the sake of brevity, I will state that in 1920 Charles Garland was a quirky, twenty-one year old son of a Wall Street banker who refused to accept a one million dollar inheritance from the estate of his

deceased father. Garland indicated to a reporter that he was not refusing to accept the inheritance because of Socialist beliefs, but rather because as part of the teachings of Jesus Christ and the workers of Lev Tolstoy, he had come to the earnest belief that the money was not his.

Hearing of this decision and the rationale, the Socialist author Upton Sinclair urged Garland to accept the money and put it to a "higher" use. Sinclair suggested making a one hundred thousand dollar donation to a set of specific organizations seeking to change the economic and social system of which Garland disapproved. Note the following organization favored by Upton Sinclair:

1. *The Liberator Magazine.*
2. The Socialist daily newspaper, *The New York Call.*
3. The Communist daily newspaper, *The Daily Worker.*
4. The Federated Press news service.
5. The Intercollegiate Socialist Society.
6. The American Civil Liberties Union.
7. The American Union Against Militarism
8. The magazine *Reconstruction* edited by the 1916 Socialist Party Presidential Candidate, Allan L. Benson.

While Garland did not accept Sinclair's suggestion, it seemed as though the idea of accepting the inheritance in the name of establishing a radical philanthropic organization was firmly planted in his head.

In 1921, Garland was approached by the Socialist Roger Baldwin, head of the American Civil Liberties Union and Walter Nelles, the attorney for the ACLU Baldwin convinced Garland to accept his father's inheritance and to establish with it a "national trust fund" which would aid efforts to expand "individual liberty and the power of voluntary association."

On July, 1921, the American Fund for Public Service was formed. The Garland money behind the fund was held in the form of securities at the (what else?) First National Bank of New York. The board of directors consisted entirely of Socialists and Communists, with Roger Baldwin leading the way.

Brookwood Labor College was listed as the first organization to receive monetary assistance for the fund. It is also interesting to note that A.J. Muste was an early supporter and worker with Roger Baldwin while forming the American Civil Liberties Union. Also, Muste taught at Brentwood Labor College from 1921-1933.

[23] The American Workers Party, not to be confused with the Workers Party of America, 1921-1929, was formed in December 1933 by activists in the Conference for Progressive Labor Action. The leader of the American Workers Party was none other than A.J. Muste who we discussed in the preceding paragraph.

The American Workers Party sought to find what it called "an American approach" for Marxism at the depth of the Great Depression; The Party published a popular newspaper called Labor Action and created Unemployment Leagues that attracted tens of thousands of members and should not be confused with the Communist Party Unemployment Councils.

The American Workers Party is best known in labor history for the leadership of the successful 1934 Toledo Auto-Lite Strike, a forerunner that contributed to the creation of the United Auto Workers Union. Exerting influence through it Unemployment League chapters, the AWP kept the Auto-Lite Strike from being broken by desperate job seekers. Instead, the AWP brought the mass of unemployed to near as a powerful vehicle for solidarity with the auto parts factory workers on the picket lines.

[24] "During 1946-1947 in any Congress of Industrial Organization meeting, moves by people such as Cary or Jacob Potofsky to criticize Soviet behavior and the end endorse American Country Measures drew sharp criticism from the strong Pro-Soviet faction. Meanwhile, in such CIO affiliates as the United Auto Workers and the Wine, Mill Workers, Anti-Communist forces began a series of bitter battles with groups and leaders charges with being Pro-Communist for control of key locals, staff positions, and even (as in the case of the UE) the union itself."

IMMIGRATION AND LABOR UNIONS ➤

[25] "By 1948 the CIO was seething with strife among the Pro-Communist and Anti-Communist groups." The Pro-Communists were inspired by the reconstitution of the Communist Party U.S.A. and proclaimed the need for labor to join a third-party effort, certain to be headed by former President Henry A. Wallace. Despite a January 1948 executive board resolution rejecting third-party politics, prominent leaders in the UE, ILWU, Wine, Moll Workers, and other Pro-Soviet affiliates announced for Wallace. So did Lee Pressman, who left his position as general counsel and thus ended an association with the CIO that went back to 1936.

[26] "During the Cold War (1945-1991) labor leaders such as Walter Reuter worked to purge Communists from the unions. Because of this Anti-American crusade and because of his effort to rid union corruption, Reuter often was a target of violence. In April 1948, he was shot at in his own kitchen window, severely injuring his right arm."

As I wind up our study of the United States Labor Unions, I hope I have given you good insight on both sides of the issue. I am sure I have provided information which is foreign to you since most of it is not included in current college textbooks. Professors, even if inclined to properly present unbiased material, are not allowed to do so. You must remember that our education system began to be deliberately controlled with the importation of Socialist professors during the nineteenth and twentieth centuries. It was gradually controlled until the late 1930s and has progressed very rapidly since then.

There definitely is a need for worker protection through representation. Without protection, management would without doubt take advantage of workers in a variety of ways. In this sense, I am Pro-Union. However, I am Anti-Union Leadership because I know there is still a great deal of Socialism and Communism among union leaders. I do not approve of the power union leaders have in political matters. They use membership dues to abundantly support Congressmen and Presidential Candidates who present the most Socialistic agendas. For example, unions contributed eight hundred million to the Obama campaign during the 2008 campaign and Democratic members are already stating that they expect much more than that for the 2012 campaign. Another tactic of union leadership is that again, by the use of membership funds, they spend heavily in brainwashing members with false information on the candidate(s) that are more conservative.

We must also remember that unions have never created a job except within the union. Staff and leadership positions within a union are grossly overpaid by the members' dues which is completely unfair. Currently, many union members are beginning to wake up to the tactics of their leaders. With the new age of mass electronic media, they are becoming better informed and see where they are being duped. Sometime in the future I believe the membership will overturn the system and will form a professional association that better suits their needs. This is especially true since membership in trade unions is declining while state and federal employee unions are on the rise.

CHAPTER 5

The American Civil Liberties Union

TODAY THE AMERICAN Civil Liberties Union presents itself as a protector of civil rights. Its stated mission is [1] "to defend and preserve the individual rights and liberties guaranteed to ever person in this country by the Constitution and laws of the United States." The American Civil Liberties Union works through litigation, legislation, and community education which covers a wide range of cases.

After forty-three years of studying the ACLU, I am convinced that the front put up by this evil and dangerous organization is absolutely false. To fully understand the details of what the American Civil Liberties Union really is, we must go back in time and look at how it was formed, why it was formed, and the background and beliefs of those who formed it. While discovering the foregoing, you must keep in mind that the American Civil Liberties Union has not changed from the day it was formed except that it has tried to dress up and appear legitimate. The primary founder of the American Civil Liberties Union, Roger Baldwin stated, "We are for Socialism, disarmament, and ultimately for abolishing the state itself ... we seek the social ownership of property, the abolition of the propertied class and the sole control of those who produce wealth. Communism is the goal." THIS IS STILL THEIR GOAL. In all the data I have assembled and analyzed, I cannot find where the American Civil Liberties Union has officially changed this position.

◄ ONCE THERE WAS AN AMERICA

From our previous discussion on the immigration and labor unions movement, you will recall the turmoil of the latter part of the nineteenth century and the twentieth century. Prior to and after the United States entry into World War I, there was an outburst of strikes, race riots, and Anarchist bombings in several cities. Also included in these radical activities was the Anti-Military Movement.

Like future generations, especially the Viet Nam War generation, there were [3] "some Americans who were opposed to the United States involvement in the war and mandatory draft. In 1915, a group of Pacifists in New York formed the American Union Against Militarism (AUAM) to work against this through political activity and the publication of anti-war newsletters, magazines, and leaflets." This organization was the precursor to the American Civil Liberties Union.

Although the American Union Against Militarism was supposedly a Pacifist group, its membership was Anarchists, Socialists, Communists, and practically every known Anti-American group. Even though she was never given full credit, Crystal Eastman was the prime organizer of AUAM. Working beside her was none other than Roger Nash Baldwin, the best known Socialist/Communist organizers in the United States.

Despite their efforts, any kind of dissent against the war was deemed unpatriotic and dangerous. President Woodrow Wilson (although a closer socialist himself) said "the authority to exercise censorship is absolutely necessary to the public safety." President Theodore Roosevelt called the anti-war advocates "enemies at home." Crystal Eastman and Roger Baldwin – both Socialists and supporters of the radical Leftist movements – formed a group within the American Union Against Militarism to assist with the large costs of those who had been prosecuted, fined, or imprisoned for printing or saying things that were against war. The AUAM split because of Eastman's and Baldwin's association with the so-called radical groups. As a result, in 1917, [4] Eastman and Baldwin merged the two groups, thereby forming the Civil Liberties Bureau and later changing the name to the National Civil Liberties Bureau.

THE AMERICAN CIVIL LIBERTIES UNION ➤

Baldwin and Eastman were not alone in forming the American Civil Liberties Union. They called in the better known Socialists, Communists, Anarchists and radicals of every known stripe to the first organization meeting. Among these radicals were William Z. Foster, Rabbi Stephen Wise, A.J. Muste, Scott Nearing, Norman Thomas, Adolph Berle, Jane Addams (future Communist Party Chairman), Max Nearing, Elizabeth Gurley Flynn, and Soviet agent, Agnes Smelly.

After refusing to comply with a draft notice for examination, Baldwin served a year in prison at the Federal Penitentiary in Atlanta, Georgia. Upon his release, Baldwin headed up a reconstructed National Civil Liberties Bureau, now the American Civil Liberties Union. The ACLU's official birth was January 19, 1920 and Roger Baldwin served as Executive Director until 1950.

Before looking at some official United States Government Investigations into the American Civil Liberties Union, I would like to present two quotes by Roger Baldwin, the still idolized leader of this Socialist/Communist organization.

As a young man graduating from college, Baldwin wrote the following in his yearbook: "I have traveled to Europe several times, mostly in connection with international radical activities ... and have traveled in the United States to areas of conflict over worker rights to strike and organize. My chief aversion is the system of greed, private profit, privilege, and violence which make up the control of the world today, and which has brought it to the tragic crises of unprecedented hunger and unemployment ... therefore, I am for Socialism, disarmament and ultimately, for the abolishing of the State itself ... I seek the social ownership of property, the abolition of the propertied class and sole control of those who produce wealth. Communism is the goal." If you turn back to the currently stated goal of the American Civil Liberties Union, you will see a near verbatim version of this yearbook quote.

The following quote by Baldwin was given to Louis Lechner of the Socialist Peoples Council in Minnesota during a meeting in 1917. [6] "Do steer away from making it look like a Socialist enterprise ... we want also to look like patriots in everything we do. We want to get a good lot of flags, talk a good deal about the Constitution and what our forefathers want to make of this country, and to show that we are really the folks that really stand for the spirit of our institutions." This tactic is still used today, as we will see later.

[7] The Joint Legislative Committee to Investigate Seditious Acts, later known as the Lusk Committee, was formed in 1919 by the New York State Legislature to investigate individuals and organizations suspected of sedition. For more than a year, the Lusk Committee gathered information on suspected radical groups raiding offices and examining documents. They also infiltrated meetings and assisted law enforcement agents in thousands of arrests and subpoenaing witnesses to testify at the Committee hearings.

In 1920, the Lusk Committee reported, [8] "There are a large number of groups in this country engaged in an effort to undermine our institutions, to weaken property rights and to set up in place of government by the majority, a government controlled by a militant minority ... at the present time, these advocates of free speech have consolidated their energies in an organization known as the American Civil Liberties Union ... [which] in the last analysis, is a supporter of all subversive movements, and its propaganda and is detrimental to the interests of the State. It attempts not only to protect crime but to encourage attacks upon our institutions in every form."

[9] The Bridgman Convention was held in August 1922 in the small town of Bridgman, Michigan about ninety miles from Chicago. This convention was called by the Communist Party of America and was attended by the top Communists, Socialists, and other radicals living in the United States.

An employee of the Bureau of Investigation (later named FBI) had infiltrated the Communist Party of America and informed his supervisor of the date and location of the gathering. The convention was raided by Federal and local law enforcement authorities on August 22, 1922. Journalists called the raid "the most colossal conspiracy

THE AMERICAN CIVIL LIBERTIES UNION

against the United State in its history." The raid resulted in the arrest or indictment of every top leader of the Communist Party of America. Naturally, the American Civil Liberties Union came to their rescue. Years later Ben Gillow wrote: "Because of the A.C.L.U. not one of the leaders served time."

The Fish Committee Report of 1931 concluded. The American Civil Liberties Union is closely affiliated with the Communist/Socialist movement in the United States and fully ninety percent of its efforts are on behalf of subversives who have come into conflict with the law. It claims to stand for free speech, free press and free assembly, but it is quite apparent that the main function of the American Civil Liberties Union is to protect subversives in their advocacy of force and violence to overthrow the government.

[10] The House Committee on Un-American Activities, also known as the House Un-American Activities Committee, was formed on 1938 as an investigative committee of the United States House of Representatives. In 1969, the House changed the committee's name to "House Committee on Internal Security." When the House abolished the committee in 1975, its functions were transferred to the House Judiciary Committee.

[11] A 1938 report from the investigation of Un-American Propaganda was presented before the Special Committee on Un-American Activities. The following is part of the report:

"Not only does the American Civil Liberties Union admit its open defense of Communists ... but it also admits that it has loaned considerable money to the International Labor Defense, a Communist movement, which is a branch of the 'Red' International aid of Russia ..."

[12] Appendix IV of the 1955 Dies Committee Report to Congress states: "In the thirty-seven years of history of the Communist Party Movement in the United States, the Communist Party has never been able to do as much for itself as the American Civil Liberties Union has done for it."

Many more cases, to include those that are more recent, can easily be presented. However, I believe you have read enough to clearly see what the American Civil Liberties Union really is and what its final is/was. That being the change of our Constitutional form of government with its free enterprise system to a Socialist form of government. Even though the officials of the ACLU are well-educated, highly intelligent, innovative, crafty, and shifty, they are too darn dumb to realize that Socialism has been a failure wherever and whenever imposed.

[13] In respect to the period we have been studying, we must again remind ourselves that other forces were at work to undermine our form of government. Socialist educators were now being "produced" in the United States, stemming from those professors who were avidly assisted in immigrating to the United States in the 1800s. With their minds on more open, subversive activities, our politicians and population in general did not realize our entire educational system was being taken over by avid Socialists. The earliest infiltration was in our Ivy League schools and in time spread to state universities. Yes! Our Seminaries were also infiltrated and by the early 1930s, it crept into our high schools and now even into pre-kindergarten. There will be more on our educational system. Also during this period, radicals were rushing to the Democratic Party who received them with open arms and assisted them in finding jobs and housing.

The Democratic Party also organized them into precincts and blocks. Each block had a captain who turned the residents out to vote for the Democratic Party in every local, state, and national election. To a great extent, this scheme continues today and is similar to the labor union scheme.

Through brainwashing by our education system, the biased mainstream media, religious institutions and especially lack of concern of our population and politicians, the American Civil Liberties Union has become a respectful organization by a large percentage of our citizens. Make no mistake, they are still the same slimy imitation of humanity that they have always been.

We know the ACLU had never deviated from its original goal, but it is presented by the academic community and the mainstream

THE AMERICAN CIVIL LIBERTIES UNION

media as an organization consisting of two separate non-profit organizations: the ACLU Foundation, a 501 (c)(d) organization which focuses on litigation and communication efforts and the American Civil Liberties Union, a 501 (c)(4) organization which focuses on legislative lobbying. Only in America could a subversive organization be allowed such privileges.

The American Civil Liberties Union has more than five million members, more than two hundred paid attorneys, over five hundred volunteer (pro bono) attorneys, and a huge staff at the national office in New York. In addition, there are dozens of branch offices located throughout the United States. At any given time, the American Civil Liberties Union handles more than six thousand cases. Guess who pays for much of these costs? Thank the Congressmen who approved the Civil Rights Attorney's Fee Awards Act of 1976. Oh! I almost forgot, the annual budget of the ACLU is between fifteen and twenty million dollars.

The American Civil Liberties Union will never change its primary objective, but my personal belief is that they heavily concentrate on the destruction of our basic institutions – especially the homes, the schools, and the churches with particular emphasis on Christian churches.

[14] The following are some of the stated goals of the American Civil Liberties Union, from their own published Policy Issues:

The legalization of prostitution.

The defense of all pornography, including child porn, as free speech.

The decriminalization and legalization of all drugs.

The promotion of homosexuality.

The opposition of rating of movies and music.

The opposition of parental consent of minors seeking abortion.

ONCE THERE WAS AN AMERICA

The opposition of informed consent preceding abortion procedures.

The opposition of espousal consent preceding abortion.

The opposition of parent choice in children's education.

We can add to the foregoing: the defense and promotion of euthanasia, polygamy, government control of religious institutions, gun control, tax-funded abortions, and birth limitations.

I believe that enough has been said about the American Civil Liberties Union but there is more. You only have to look for it.

CHAPTER 6

The Constitution of the United States of America

WE ARE AT the point where we need to look closely at the most magnificent document ever written: The Constitution of the United States and the Declaration of Independence. Perhaps I should have included it prior to covering subjects like the Federal Reserve System and the American Civil Liberties Union. Instead, I chose to place it near the center since we definitely will need knowledge of it for the forthcoming subjects.

Most American citizens have never read the Constitution and certainly will not take the time to purchase one from a bookstore or the United States Government Printing Office. As a result, they know little about this great work of our forefathers. How many times have you heard someone argue that the Constitution gives him or her rights of life, liberty, and the pursuit of happiness? These rights are not in the Constitution, they are in the Declaration of Independence. How many of you know the Bill of Rights is the first Ten Amendments to the Constitution? I hope you get my point. We are in perilous times and the knowledge and use of the Constitution along with beliefs in God can be our savior.

◄ ONCE THERE WAS AN AMERICA

¹ THE DECLARATION OF INDEPENDENCE

When in the course of human events, it becomes necessary for one People to dissolve the Political Bands which have connected them with another, and to assume among the Powers of the Earth, the separate but equal Station to which the Laws of Nature and of Nature's God entitle them, a decent Respect to the Opinion of Mankind requires that they should declare the causes which impel them to the Separation.

We hold these Truths to be self-evident, that all Men are created equal, that they are endowed by their Creator with certain unalienable Rights, that among these are Life, Liberty, and the Pursuit of Happiness. That to secure these Rights, Governments are instituted among Men, deriving their just Powers from the Consent of the Government. That whenever any form of Government becomes destructive of these Ends, it is the Right of the people to alter or to abolish it, and to institute new Government, laying its Foundation on such Principles, and organizing its Powers in such Form, as to them shall seem most likely to affect their Safety and Happiness. Prudence, indeed will dictate the Governments long established should not be changed for light and transient Causes; and accordingly, all Experience has shown, that Mankind are more disposed to suffer, while Evils are sufferable, than Abuse and Usurpations, pursuing invariably the same Object, evinces a Design to reduce them under absolute Despotism, it is their Right, it is their Duty, to throw off such Government, and to provide new Guards for their future Security. Such has been the patient Sufferances of these Colonies, and such is now the Necessity which constrains them to alter their former System of Government. The History of the present King of Great Britain is a history of repeated Injuries and Usurpation all having in direct Object the Establishment of an absolute Tyranny over these States. To prove this, let Facts be submitted to a candid World.

He has refused his Assent to Laws, the most wholesome and necessary for the public Good.

He has forbidden his Government to pass Laws of immediate

and pressing importance, unless suspended in their Operation till his Assent should be obtained; and when so suspended, he has utterly neglected to attend to them.

He has refused to pass other Laws for the Accommodation of large Districts of People, unless those People would relinquish the Right of Representation in the Legislature, a Right inestimable to them and formidable to Tyrants only.

He has called together Legislative Bodies at Places unusual, uncomfortable, and distant from the Depository of their public Records for the sole Purpose of fatiguing them into Compliance with his Measures.

He has dissolved Representative Houses repeatedly, for opposing with manly Firmness his Invasion on the Rights of the People.

He has refused for a long Time, after such Dissolutions, to cause others to be elected; whereby the Legislative Powers, incapable of Annihilation, have returned to the People at large for their exercise, the State remaining in the meantime exposed to all the Dangers of Invasion from without, and Convulsions within.

He has endeavored to prevent the Population of these States; for the Purpose of obstructing the Laws for Naturalization of the Foreigners, refusing to pass others to encourage their Migrations hither, and raising the Conditions of new Appropriations.

He has obstructed the Administration of Justice, by refusing his Assent to Laws for establishing Judiciary Powers.

He has made Judges dependent on his Will alone, for the Tenure of their Offices, and the Amount and Payment of their Salaries.

He has erected a Multitude of New Offices and sent higher Swarms Officers to harass our People, and eat out their Substance.

He has kept among us, in Times of Peace Standing Armies, without the Consent of our Legislatures.

He has affected to render the Military independence of and superior to the Civil Power.

He has combined with others to subject us to Jurisdictions foreign to our Constitution, and unacknowledged by our Laws, giving his

Assent to their Acts of pretended Legislation.

For quartering large Bodies of armed Troops among us;

For protecting them, by a mock Trial, from Punishment for any Murders which they should commit on the Inhabitants of these States;

For cutting off our Trade will all Parts of the World;

For imposing Taxes on us without our Consent;

For depriving us, in many Cases, of the Benefits of Trial by Jury;

For transporting us beyond Seas to be tried for pretended Offenses;

For abolishing the free System of English Laws in a neighboring Province, establishing therein an Arbitrary Government, and enlarging its Boundaries so as to render it at once an Example and fit Instrument for introducing the same absolute Rule in these Colonies;

For taking away our Charters, abolishing our most valuable Laws, and altering fundamentally the Forms of our Governments;

For suspending our own Legislatures, and declaring themselves invested with Power to legislate for us in all Cases whatsoever;

He has abdicated Government here, by declaring us out of his Protection and waging War against us.

He has plundered our Seas, ravaged our Coasts, burnt our Towns, and destroyed the Lives of our People.

He is at this time transporting large Armies of foreign Mercenaries to complete the Works of Death, Desolation and Tyranny, already begun with circumstances of Cruelty and Perfidy scarcely paralleled in the most barbarous Ages, and totally unworthy of the Head of a civilized Nation.

He has constrained our fellow Citizens taken Captive on the high Seas to bear Arms against their Country, to become the Executioners of their Friends and Brethren or to fall themselves by their Hands.

He has excited domestic Insurrection amongst us, and has endeavored to bring on the Inhabitants of our Frontiers. The merciless Indian Savages, whose known rule of warfare is an undistinguished destruction of all ages, sexes and conditions.

In every stage of these Oppressions, We have Petitioned for Redress in the most humble Terms: Our repeated Petitions have been answered only by repeated Injury. A prince, whose character is thus marked by every act which may define a Tyranny, is unfit to be Ruler of a free People.

Nor have we been wanting in attention to our British Brethren. We have warned them from time to time of attempts by their Legislature to extend an unwarrantable Jurisdiction over us. We have reminded them of the Circumstances of our Emigration to settlement here. We have appealed to their native Justice and Magnanimity, and have conjured them by the Ties of our common Kindred to disavow these Usurpations, which would inevitably interrupt our Connections and Correspondence. They too have been deaf to the Voice of Justice and of Consanguinity. We must, therefore, acquiesce in the Necessity which denounces our Separation, and hold them, as we hold the rest of Mankind, Enemies in War, in Peace, Friends.

WE, THEREFORE the REPRESENTATIVES of the UNITED STATES OF AMERICA, IN GENERAL CONGRESS, Assemble, appealing to the Supreme Judge of the world, or the rectitude of our intentions, do, in the Name, and by the authority of the good People of these Colonies, solemnly PUBLISH and DECLARE, that these United Colonies are, and of Right ought to be FREE AND INDEPENDENT STATES; that they are Absolved from all Allegiance to the British Crown and that all political connections between them and the State of Great Britain, is and ought to be totally dissolved; and that as FREE and INDEPENDENT STATES, they have full Power to levy War, conclude Peace, contract Allegiances, establish Commerce, and to do all other Acts and Things which INDEPENDENT STATES, may of right do. And for the support of this Declaration, with a firm reliance on the protection of Divine Providence, We mutually pledge to each other our Lives, our Fortunes, and our sacred Honor.

SIGNERS OF THE DECLARATION OF INDEPENDENCE
CONNECTICUT
  Roger Sherman
  Samuel Huntington

◄ ONCE THERE WAS AN AMERICA

    William Williams
    Oliver Wolcott
DELAWARE
    Caesar Rodnet
    George Read
    Thomas McLean
GEORGIA
    Button Gwinnett
    Lyman Hall
    George Walton
MARYLAND
    Samuel Chase
    William Pace
    Thomas Stone
    Charles Carroll
MASSACHUSETTS
    John Hancock
    Samuel Adams
    John Adams
    Robert Treat Paine
    Eldridge Gerry
NEW HAMPSHIRE
    Josiah Bartlett
    William Whipple
    Matthew Thornton
NEW JERSEY
    Richard Stockton
    Jonathan Witherspoon
    Francis Hopkinson
    John Hart
    Abraham Clark
NEW YORK
    William Floyd
    Phillip Livingston

THE CONSTITUTION OF THE UNITED STATES OF AMERICA

    Francis Lewis
    Lewis Morris
NORTH CAROLINA
    William Hooper
    Joseph Hewes
    John Penn
PENNSYLVANIA
    Robert Morris
    Benjamin Rush
    Benjamin Franklin
    John Morton
    George Clymer
    James Smith
    George Taylor
    James Wilson
    George Ross
RHODE ISLAND
    Stephen Hopkins
    Williams Aller
SOUTH CAROLINA
    Edward Rutledge
    Thomas Hayward, Jr.
    Thomas Lynch, Jr.
    Arthur Middletown
VIRGINIA
    George White
    Richard Henry Lee
    Thomas Jefferson
    Benjamin Harrison
    Thomas Nelson, Jr.
    Francis "Light Foot" Lee
    Carter Brixton

ONCE THERE WAS AN AMERICA

In the last chapter of this book, I offer many things you can do to get our country back. I cannot stress it strongly enough, but you must organize into the most powerful organization the United States has ever known. It will take a tremendous sacrifice on the part of millions because you will be facing the strongest, most prominent and powerful forces in the world, to include most of our own government. You must be strong, forceful, loud, brave, and unrelenting, but you MUST ALWAYS BE LEGAL. Study the Constitution with fervor because it can be your friend in many ways.

THE CONSTITUTION OF THE UNITED STATES OF AMERICA ➤

²THE UNITED STATES CONSTITUTION

We the people of the United States, in order to form a more perfect union, establish justice, insure domestic tranquility, provide for the common defense, promote the general welfare, and secure the blessings of liberty to ourselves and our posterity, do ordain and establish this Constitution for the United States of America.

Article I
SECTION 1.

All legislative powers herein granted shall be vested in a Congress of the United States, which shall consist of a Senate and House of Representatives.

SECTION 2.

Clause 1: The House of Representatives shall be composed of members chosen every second year by the people of the several states, and the electors in each state shall have the qualifications requisite for electors of the most numerous branch of the state legislature.

Clause 2: No person shall be a Representative who shall not have attained to the age of twenty five years, and been seven years a citizen of the United States, and who shall not, when elected, be an inhabitant of that state in which he shall be chosen.

Clause 3: Representatives and direct taxes shall be apportioned among the several states which may be included within this union, according to their respective numbers, which shall be determined by adding to the whole number of free persons, including those bound to service for a term of years, and excluding Indians not taxed, three fifths of all other Persons. The actual Enumeration shall be made within three years after the first meeting of the Congress of the United States, and within every subsequent term of ten years, in such manner as they shall by law direct. The number of Representatives shall not exceed one for every thirty thousand, but each state shall have at least one Representative; and until such enumeration shall be made, the state of New Hampshire shall be entitled to chuse three,

Massachusetts eight, Rhode Island and Providence Plantations one, Connecticut five, New York six, New Jersey four, Pennsylvania eight, Delaware one, Maryland six, Virginia ten, North Carolina five, South Carolina five, and Georgia three.

Clause 4: When vacancies happen in the Representation from any state, the executive authority thereof shall issue writs of election to fill such vacancies.

Clause 5: The House of Representatives shall choose their speaker and other officers; and shall have the sole power of impeachment.

SECTION 3.

Clause 1: The Senate of the United States shall be composed of two Senators from each state, chosen by the legislature thereof, for six years; and each Senator shall have one vote.

Clause 2: Immediately after they shall be assembled in consequence of the first election, they shall be divided as equally as may be into three classes. The seats of the Senators of the first class shall be vacated at the expiration of the second year, of the second class at the expiration of the fourth year, and the third class at the expiration of the sixth year, so that one third may be chosen every second year; and if vacancies happen by resignation, or otherwise, during the recess of the legislature of any state, the executive thereof may make temporary appointments until the next meeting of the legislature, which shall then fill such vacancies.

Clause 3: No person shall be a Senator who shall not have attained to the age of thirty years, and been nine years a citizen of the United States and who shall not, when elected, be an inhabitant of that state for which he shall be chosen.

Clause 4: The Vice President of the United States shall be President of the Senate, but shall have no vote, unless they be equally divided.

Clause 5: The Senate shall choose their other officers, and also a President pro tempore, in the absence of the Vice President, or when he shall exercise the office of President of the United States.

Clause 6: The Senate shall have the sole power to try all

impeachments. When sitting for that purpose, they shall be on oath or affirmation. When the President of the United States is tried, the Chief Justice shall preside: And no person shall be convicted without the concurrence of two thirds of the members present.

Clause 7: Judgment in cases of impeachment shall not extend further than to removal from office, and disqualification to hold and enjoy any office of honor, trust or profit under the United States: but the party convicted shall nevertheless be liable and subject to indictment, trial, judgment and punishment, according to law.

SECTION 4.

Clause 1: The times, places and manner of holding elections for Senators and Representatives, shall be prescribed in each state by the legislature thereof; but the Congress may at any time by law make or alter such regulations, except as to the places of choosing Senators.

Clause 2: The Congress shall assemble at least once in every year, and such meeting shall be on the first Monday in December, unless they shall by law appoint a different day.

SECTION 5.

Clause 1: Each House shall be the judge of the elections, returns and qualifications of its own members, and a majority of each shall constitute a quorum to do business; but a smaller number may adjourn from day to day, and may be authorized to compel the attendance of absent members, in such manner, and under such penalties as each House may provide.

Clause 2: Each House may determine the rules of its proceedings, punish its members for disorderly behavior, and, with the concurrence of two thirds, expel a member.

Clause 3: Each House shall keep a journal of its proceedings, and from time to time publish the same, excepting such parts as may in their judgment require secrecy; and the yeas and nays of the members of either House on any question shall, at the desire of one fifth of those present, be entered on the journal.

Clause 4: Neither House, during the session of Congress, shall, without the consent of the other, adjourn for more than three days, nor to any other place than that in which the two Houses shall be sitting.

SECTION 6.

Clause 1: The Senators and Representatives shall receive a compensation for their services, to be ascertained by law, and paid out of the treasury of the United States. They shall in all cases, except treason, felony and breach of the peace, be privileged from arrest during their attendance at the session of their respective Houses, and in going to and returning from the same; and for any speech or debate in either House, they shall not be questioned in any other place.

Clause 2: No Senator or Representative shall, during the time for which he was elected, be appointed to any civil office under the authority of the United States, which shall have been created, or the emoluments whereof shall have been increased during such time: and no person holding any office under the United States, shall be a member of either House during his continuance in office.

SECTION 7.

Clause 1: All bills for raising revenue shall originate in the House of Representatives; but the Senate may propose or concur with amendments as on other Bills.

Clause 2: Every bill which shall have passed the House of Representatives and the Senate, shall, before it become a law, be presented to the President of the United States; if he approve he shall sign it, but if not he shall return it, with his objections to that House in which it shall have originated, who shall enter the objections at large on their journal, and proceed to reconsider it. If after such reconsideration two thirds of that House shall agree to pass the bill, it shall be sent, together with the objections, to the other House, by which it shall likewise be reconsidered, and if approved by two thirds of that House, it shall become a law. But in all such cases the votes of both

THE CONSTITUTION OF THE UNITED STATES OF AMERICA

Houses shall be determined by yeas and nays, and the names of the persons voting for and against the bill shall be entered on the journal of each House respectively. If any bill shall not be returned by the President within ten days (Sundays excepted) after it shall have been presented to him, the same shall be a law, in like manner as if he had signed it, unless the Congress by their adjournment prevent its return, in which case it shall not be a law.

Clause 3: Every order, resolution, or vote to which the concurrence of the Senate and House of Representatives may be necessary (except on a question of adjournment) shall be presented to the President of the United States; and before the same shall take effect, shall be approved by him, or being disapproved by him, shall be repassed by two thirds of the Senate and House of Representatives, according to the rules and limitations prescribed in the case of a bill.

SECTION 8.

Clause 1: The Congress shall have power to lay and collect taxes, duties, imposts and excises, to pay the debts and provide for the common defense and general welfare of the United States; but all duties, imposts and excises shall be uniform throughout the United States;

Clause 2: To borrow money on the credit of the United States;

Clause 3: To regulate commerce with foreign nations, and among the several states, and with the Indian tribes;

Clause 4: To establish a uniform rule of naturalization, and uniform laws on the subject of bankruptcies throughout the United States;

Clause 5: To coin money, regulate the value thereof, and of foreign coin, and fix the standard of weights and measures;

Clause 6: To provide for the punishment of counterfeiting the securities and current coin of the United States;

Clause 7: To establish post offices and post roads;

Clause 8: To promote the progress of science and useful arts, by securing for limited times to authors and inventors the exclusive right to their respective writings and discoveries;

Clause 9: To constitute tribunals inferior to the Supreme Court;

Clause 10: To define and punish piracies and felonies committed on the high seas, and offenses against the law of nations;

Clause 11: To declare war, grant letters of marque and reprisal, and make rules concerning captures on land and water;

Clause 12: To raise and support armies, but no appropriation of money to that use shall be for a longer term than two years;

Clause 13: To provide and maintain a navy;

Clause 14: To make rules for the government and regulation of the land and naval forces;

Clause 15: To provide for calling forth the militia to execute the laws of the union, suppress insurrections and repel invasions;

Clause 16: To provide for organizing, arming, and disciplining, the militia, and for governing such part of them as may be employed in the service of the United States, reserving to the states respectively, the appointment of the officers, and the authority of training the militia according to the discipline prescribed by Congress;

Clause 17: To exercise exclusive legislation in all cases whatsoever, over such District (not exceeding ten miles square) as may, by cession of particular states, and the acceptance of Congress, become the seat of the government of the United States, and to exercise like authority over all places purchased by the consent of the legislature of the state in which the same shall be, for the erection of forts, magazines, arsenals, dockyards, and other needful buildings;

Clause 18: And To make all laws which shall be necessary and proper for carrying into execution the foregoing powers, and all other powers vested by this Constitution in the government of the United States, or in any department or officer thereof.

SECTION 9.

Clause 1: The migration or importation of such persons as any of the states now existing shall think proper to admit, shall not be prohibited by the Congress prior to the year one thousand eight hundred and eight, but a tax or duty may be imposed on such importation, not exceeding ten dollars for each person.

Clause 2: The privilege of the writ of habeas corpus shall not be suspended, unless when in cases of rebellion or invasion the public safety may require it.

Clause 3: No bill of attainder or ex post facto Law shall be passed.

Clause 4: No capitation, or other direct, tax shall be laid, unless in proportion to the census or enumeration herein before directed to be taken.

Clause 5: No tax or duty shall be laid on articles exported from any state.

Clause 6: No preference shall be given by any regulation of commerce or revenue to the ports of one state over those of another: nor shall vessels bound to, or from, one state, be obliged to enter, clear or pay duties in another.

Clause 7: No money shall be drawn from the treasury, but in consequence of appropriations made by law; and a regular statement and account of receipts and expenditures of all public money shall be published from time to time.

Clause 8: No title of nobility shall be granted by the United States: and no person holding any office of profit or trust under them, shall, without the consent of the Congress, accept of any present, emolument, office, or title, of any kind whatever, from any king, prince, or foreign state.

SECTION 10.

Clause 1: No state shall enter into any treaty, alliance, or confederation; grant letters of marque and reprisal; coin money; emit bills of credit; make anything but gold and silver coin a tender in payment of debts; pass any bill of attainder, ex post facto law, or law impairing the obligation of contracts, or grant any title of nobility.

Clause 2: No state shall, without the consent of the Congress, lay any imposts or duties on imports or exports, except what may be absolutely necessary for executing its inspection laws: and the net produce of all duties and imposts, laid by any state on imports or exports, shall be for the use of the treasury of the United States; and all such laws shall be subject to the revision and control of the Congress.

Clause 3: No state shall, without the consent of Congress, lay any duty of tonnage, keep troops, or ships of war in time of peace, enter into any agreement or compact with another state, or with a foreign power, or engage in war, unless actually invaded, or in such imminent danger as will not admit of delay.

Article II

SECTION 1.

Clause 1: The executive power shall be vested in a President of the United States of America. He shall hold his office during the term of four years, and, together with the Vice President, chosen for the same term, be elected, as follows:

Clause 2: Each state shall appoint, in such manner as the Legislature thereof may direct, a number of electors, equal to the whole number of Senators and Representatives to which the State may be entitled in the Congress: but no Senator or Representative, or person holding an office of trust or profit under the United States, shall be appointed an elector.

Clause 3: The electors shall meet in their respective states, and vote by ballot for two persons, of whom one at least shall not be an inhabitant of the same state with themselves. And they shall make a list of all the persons voted for, and of the number of votes for each; which list they shall sign and certify, and transmit sealed to the seat of the government of the United States, directed to the President of the Senate. The President of the Senate shall, in the presence of the Senate and House of Representatives, open all the certificates, and the votes shall then be counted. The person having the greatest number of votes shall be the President, if such number be a majority of the whole number of electors appointed; and if there be more than one who have such majority, and have an equal number of votes, then the House of Representatives shall immediately choose by ballot one of them for President; and if no person have a majority, then from the

THE CONSTITUTION OF THE UNITED STATES OF AMERICA

five highest on the list the said House shall in like manner choose the President. But in choosing the President, the votes shall be taken by States, the representation from each state having one vote; A quorum for this purpose shall consist of a member or members from two thirds of the states, and a majority of all the states shall be necessary to a choice. In every case, after the choice of the President, the person having the greatest number of votes of the electors shall be the Vice President. But if there should remain two or more who have equal votes, the Senate shall choose from them by ballot the Vice President.

Clause 4: The Congress may determine the time of choosing the electors, and the day on which they shall give their votes; which day shall be the same throughout the United States.

Clause 5: No person except a natural born citizen, or a citizen of the United States, at the time of the adoption of this Constitution, shall be eligible to the office of President; neither shall any person be eligible to that office who shall not have attained to the age of thirty five years, and been fourteen Years a resident within the United States.

Clause 6: In case of the removal of the President from office, or of his death, resignation, or inability to discharge the powers and duties of the said office, the same shall devolve on the Vice President, and the Congress may by law provide for the case of removal, death, resignation or inability, both of the President and Vice President, declaring what officer shall then act as President, and such officer shall act accordingly, until the disability be removed, or a President shall be elected.

Clause 7: The President shall, at stated times, receive for his services, a compensation, which shall neither be increased nor diminished during the period for which he shall have been elected, and he shall not receive within that period any other emolument from the United States, or any of them.

Clause 8: Before he enter on the execution of his office, he shall take the following oath or affirmation:--I do solemnly swear (or affirm) that I will faithfully execute the office of President of the United States, and will to the best of my ability, preserve, protect and defend the Constitution of the United States.

SECTION 2.

Clause 1: The President shall be commander in chief of the Army and Navy of the United States, and of the militia of the several states, when called into the actual service of the United States; he may require the opinion, in writing, of the principal officer in each of the executive departments, upon any subject relating to the duties of their respective offices, and he shall have power to grant reprieves and pardons for offenses against the United States, except in cases of impeachment.

Clause 2: He shall have power, by and with the advice and consent of the Senate, to make

treaties, provided two thirds of the Senators present concur; and he shall nominate, and by and with the advice and consent of the Senate, shall appoint ambassadors, other public ministers and consuls, judges of the Supreme Court, and all other officers of the United States, whose appointments are not herein otherwise provided for, and which shall be established by law: but the Congress may by law vest the appointment of such inferior officers, as they think proper, in the President alone, in the courts of law, or in the heads of departments.

Clause 3: The President shall have power to fill up all vacancies that may happen during the recess of the Senate, by granting commissions which shall expire at the end of their next session.

SECTION 3.

He shall from time to time give to the Congress information of the state of the union, and recommend to their consideration such measures as he shall judge necessary and expedient; he may, on extraordinary occasions, convene both Houses, or either of them, and in case of disagreement between them, with respect to the time of adjournment, he may adjourn them to such time as he shall think proper; he shall receive ambassadors and other public ministers; he shall take care that the laws be faithfully executed, and shall commission all the officers of the United States.

SECTION 4.
The President, Vice President and all civil officers of the United States, shall be removed from office on impeachment for, and conviction of, treason, bribery, or other high crimes and misdemeanors.

Article III

SECTION 1.
The judicial power of the United States, shall be vested in one Supreme Court, and in such inferior courts as the Congress may from time to time ordain and establish. The judges, both of the supreme and inferior courts, shall hold their offices during good behaviour, and shall, at stated times, receive for their services, a compensation, which shall not be diminished during their continuance in office.

SECTION 2.
Clause 1: The judicial power shall extend to all cases, in law and equity, arising under this Constitution, the laws of the United States, and treaties made, or which shall be made, under their authority;--to all cases affecting ambassadors, other public ministers and consuls;--to all cases ofadmiralty and maritime jurisdiction;--to controversies to which the United States shall be a party;--to controversies between two or more states;--between a state and citizens of another state;--between citizens of different states;--between citizens of the same state claiming lands under grants of different states, and between a state, or the citizens thereof, and foreign states, citizens or subjects.

Clause 2: In all cases affecting ambassadors, other public ministers and consuls, and those in which a state shall be party, the Supreme Court shall have original jurisdiction. In all the other cases before mentioned, the Supreme Court shall have appellate jurisdiction, both as to law and fact, with such exceptions, and under such regulations as the Congress shall make.

Clause 3: The trial of all crimes, except in cases of impeachment, shall be by jury; and such trial shall be held in the state where the said crimes shall have been committed; but when not committed within any state, the trial shall be at such place or places as the Congress may by law have directed.

SECTION 3.
Clause 1: Treason against the United States, shall consist only in levying war against them, or in adhering to their enemies, giving them aid and comfort. No person shall be convicted of treason unless on the testimony of two witnesses to the same overt act, or on confession in open court.

Clause 2: The Congress shall have power to declare the punishment of treason, but no attainder of treason shall work corruption of blood, or forfeiture except during the life of the person attainted.

Article IV

SECTION 1.
Full faith and credit shall be given in each state to the public acts, records, and judicial proceedings of every other state. And the Congress may by general laws prescribe the manner in which such acts, records, and proceedings shall be proved, and the effect thereof.

SECTION 2.
Clause 1: The citizens of each state shall be entitled to all privileges and immunities of citizens in the several states.

Clause 2: A person charged in any state with treason, felony, or other crime, who shall flee from justice, and be found in another state, shall on demand of the executive authority of the state from which he fled, be delivered up, to be removed to the state having jurisdiction of the crime.

Clause 3: No person held to service or labor in one state, under the laws thereof, escaping into another, shall, in consequence of any law or regulation therein, be discharged from such service or labor, but shall be delivered up on claim of the party to whom such service or labor may be due.

SECTION 3.

Clause 1: New states may be admitted by the Congress into this union; but no new states shall be formed or erected within the jurisdiction of any other state; nor any state be formed by the junction of two or more states, or parts of states, without the consent of the legislatures of the states concerned as well as of the Congress.

Clause 2: The Congress shall have power to dispose of and make all needful rules and regulations respecting the territory or other property belonging to the United States; and nothing in this Constitution shall be so construed as to prejudice any claims of the United States, or of any particular state.

SECTION 4.

The United States shall guarantee to every state in this union a republican form of government, and shall protect each of them against invasion; and on application of the legislature, or of the executive (when the legislature cannot be convened) against domestic violence.

Article V

The Congress, whenever two thirds of both houses shall deem it necessary, shall propose amendments to this Constitution, or, on the application of the legislatures of two thirds of the several states, shall call a convention for proposing amendments, which, in either case, shall be valid to all intents and purposes, as part of this Constitution, when ratified by the legislatures of three fourths of the several states, or by conventions in three fourths thereof, as the one or the other mode of ratification may be proposed by the Congress; provided that no amendment which may be made prior to the year one thousand eight hundred and eight shall in any manner affect the first and fourth clauses in the ninth section of the first article; and that no state, without its consent, shall be deprived of its equal suffrage in the Senate.

Article VI

Clause 1: All debts contracted and engagements entered into, before the adoption of this Constitution, shall be as valid against the United States under this Constitution, as under the Confederation.

Clause 2: This Constitution, and the laws of the United States which shall be made in pursuance thereof; and all treaties made, or which shall be made, under the authority of the United States, shall be the supreme law of the land; and the judges in every state shall be bound thereby, anything in the Constitution or laws of any State to the contrary notwithstanding.

Clause 3: The Senators and Representatives before mentioned, and the members of the several state legislatures, and all executive and judicial officers, both of the United States and of the several states, shall be bound by oath or affirmation, to support this Constitution; but no religious test shall ever be required as a qualification to any office or public trust under the United States.

Article VII

The ratification of the conventions of nine states, shall be sufficient for the establishment of this Constitution between the states so ratifying the same.

Done in convention by the unanimous consent of the states present the seventeenth day of September in the year of our Lord one thousand seven hundred and eighty seven and of the independence of the United States of America the twelfth. In witness whereof We have hereunto subscribed our Names, G. Washington-President and deputy from Virginia

NEW HAMPSHIRE
John Langdon
Nicholas Gilman

THE CONSTITUTION OF THE UNITED STATES OF AMERICA

MASSACHUSETTS
- Nathaniel Gorham
- Rufus King

CONNECTICUT
- Wm: Saml. Johnson
- Roger Sherman

NEW YORK
- Alexander Hamilton
- Educating Young People about the Constitution

NEW JERSEY
- Wil: Livingston
- David Brearly
- Wm. Paterson
- Jona: Dayton

PENNSYLVANIA
- B. Franklin
- Thomas Mifflin
- Robt. Morris
- Geo. Clymer
- Thos. FitzSimons
- Jared Ingersoll
- James Wilson
- Gouv Morris

DELAWARE
- Geo: Read
- Gunning Bedford jun
- John Dickinson
- Richard Bassett
- Jaco: Broom

MARYLAND
- James McHenry
- Dan of St Thos. Jenifer
- Danl Carroll

VIRGINIA
  John Blair—
  James Madison Jr.
NORTH CAROLINA
  Wm. Blount
  Richd. Dobbs Spaight
  Hu Williamson
SOUTH CAROLINA
  J. Rutledge
  Charles Cotesworth Pinckney
  Charles Pinckney
  Pierce Butler
GEORGIA
  William Few
  Abr Baldwin

The Conventions of a number of the States having, at the time of adopting the Constitution, expressed a desire, in order to prevent misconstruction or abuse of its powers, that further declaratory and restrictive clauses should be added, and as extending the ground of public confidence in the Government will best insure the beneficent ends of its institution; Resolved, by the Senate and House of Representatives of the United States of America, in Congress assembled, two-thirds of both Houses concurring, that the following articles be proposed to the Legislatures of the several States, as amendments to the Constitution of the United States; all or any of which articles, when ratified by three-fourths of the said Legislatures, to be valid to all intents and purposes as part of the said Constitution, namely:

[3]Amendment I

Congress shall make no law respecting an establishment of religion, or prohibiting the free exercise thereof; or abridging the freedom of speech, or of the press; or the right of the people peaceably to assemble, and to petition the government for a redress of grievances.

Amendment II

A well-regulated militia, being necessary to the security of a free state, the right of the people to keep and bear arms, shall not be infringed.

Amendment III

No soldier shall, in time of peace be quartered in any house, without the consent of the owner, nor in time of war, but in a manner to be prescribed by law.

Amendment IV

The right of the people to be secure in their persons, houses, papers, and effects, against unreasonable searches and seizures, shall not be violated, and no warrants shall issue, but upon probable cause, supported by oath or affirmation, and particularly describing the place to be searched, and the persons or things to be seized.

Amendment V

No person shall be held to answer for a capital, or otherwise infamous crime, unless on a presentment or indictment of a grand jury, except in cases arising in the land or naval forces, or in the militia, when in actual service in time of war or public danger; nor shall any person be subject for the same offense to be twice put in jeopardy of life or limb; nor shall be compelled in any criminal case to be a witness against himself, nor be deprived of life, liberty, or property, without due process of law; nor shall private property be taken for public use, without just compensation.

Amendment VI

In all criminal prosecutions, the accused shall enjoy the right to a speedy and public trial, by an impartial jury of the state and district wherein the crime shall have been committed, which district shall have been previously ascertained by law, and to be informed of the nature and cause of the accusation; to be confronted with the witnesses against him; to have compulsory process for obtaining witnesses in his favor, and to have the assistance of counsel for his defense.

Amendment VII

In suits at common law, where the value in controversy shall exceed twenty dollars, the right of trial by jury shall be preserved, and no fact tried by a jury, shall be otherwise reexamined in any court of the United States, than according to the rules of the common law.

Amendment VIII

Excessive bail shall not be required, nor excessive fines imposed, nor cruel and unusual punishments inflicted.

Amendment IX

The enumeration in the Constitution, of certain rights, shall not be construed to deny or disparage others retained by the people.

Amendment X

The powers not delegated to the United States by the Constitution, nor prohibited by it to the states, are reserved to the states respectively, or to the people.

Amendment XI

Passed by Congress March 4, 1794. Ratified February 7, 1795.

The judicial power of the United States shall not be construed to extend to any suit in law or equity, commenced or prosecuted against one of the United States by citizens of another state, or by citizens or subjects of any foreign state.

Amendment XII

Passed by Congress December 9, 1803. Ratified June 15, 1804.

The electors shall meet in their respective states and vote by ballot for President and Vice-President, one of whom, at least, shall not be

THE CONSTITUTION OF THE UNITED STATES OF AMERICA

an inhabitant of the same state with themselves; they shall name in their ballots the person voted for as President, and in distinct ballots the person voted for as Vice-President, and they shall make distinct lists of all persons voted for as President, and of all persons voted for as Vice-President, and of the number of votes for each, which lists they shall sign and certify, and transmit sealed to the seat of the government of the United States, directed to the President of the Senate;-- The President of the Senate shall, in the presence of the Senate and House of Representatives, open all the certificates and the votes shall then be counted;--the person having the greatest number of votes for President, shall be the President, if such number be a majority of the whole number of electors appointed; and if no person have such majority, then from the persons having the highest numbers not exceeding three on the list of those voted for as President, the House of Representatives shall choose immediately, by ballot, the President. But in choosing the President, the votes shall be taken by states, the representation from each state having one vote; a quorum for this purpose shall consist of a member or members from two-thirds of the states, and a majority of all the states shall be necessary to a choice. And if the House of Representatives shall not choose a President whenever the right of choice shall devolve upon them, before the fourth day of March next following, then the Vice-President shall act as President, as in the case of the death or other constitutional disability of the President. The person having the greatest number of votes as Vice- President, shall be the Vice-President, if such number be a majority of the whole number of electors appointed, and if no person have a majority, then from the two highest numbers on the list, the Senate shall choose the Vice-President; a quorum for the purpose shall consist of two-thirds of the whole number of Senators, and a majority of the whole number shall be necessary to a choice. But no person constitutionally ineligible to the office of President shall be eligible to that of Vice-President of the United States.

Amendment XIII

Passed by Congress January 31, 1865 Ratified December 6,1865.

Section 1.

Neither slavery nor involuntary servitude, except as a punishment for crime whereof the party shall have been duly convicted, shall exist within the United States, or anyplace subject to their jurisdiction.

Section 2.

Congress shall have power to enforce this article by appropriate legislation.

Amendment XIV

Passed by Congress June 13, 1866. Ratified July 9, 1868.

Section 1.

All persons born or naturalized in the United States, and subject to the jurisdiction thereof, are citizens of the United States and of the state wherein they reside. No state shall make or enforce any law which shall abridge the privileges or immunities of citizens of the United States; nor shall any state deprive any person of life, liberty, or property, without due process of law; nor deny to any person within its jurisdiction the equal protection of the laws.

Section 2.

Representatives shall be apportioned among the several states according to their respective numbers, counting the whole number of persons in each state, excluding Indians not taxed. But when the right to vote at any election for the choice of electors for President and Vice President of the United States, Representatives in Congress, the executive and judicial officers of a state, or the members of the legislature thereof, is denied to any of the male inhabitants of such state, being twenty-one years of age, and citizens of the United States, or in any way abridged, except for participation in rebellion, or other crime, the basis of representation therein shall be reduced in the proportion which the number of such male citizens shall bear to the whole number of male citizens twenty one years of age in such state.

Section 3.

No person shall be a Senator or Representative in Congress, or elector of President and Vice President, or hold any office, civil or military, under the United States, or under any state, who, having previously taken an oath, as a member of Congress, or as an officer of the United States, or as a member of any state legislature, or as an executive or judicial officer of any state, to support the Constitution of the United States, shall have engaged in insurrection or rebellion against the same, or given aid or comfort to the enemies thereof. But Congress may by a vote of two-thirds of each House, remove such disability.

Section 4.

The validity of the public debt of the United States, authorized by law, including debts incurred for payment of pensions and bounties for services in suppressing insurrection or rebellion, shall not be questioned. But neither the United States nor any state shall assume or pay any debt or obligation incurred in aid of insurrection or rebellion against the United States, or any claim for the loss or emancipation of any slave; but all such debts, obligations and claims shall be held illegal and void.

Section 5.

The Congress shall have power to enforce, by appropriate legislation, the provisions of this article.

Amendment XV
Passed by Congress February 26, 1869. Ratified February 3, 1870.

Section 1.
The right of citizens of the United States to vote shall not be denied or abridged by the United States or by any state on account of race, color, or previous condition of servitude.

Section 2.
The Congress shall have power to enforce this article by appropriate legislation.

Amendment XVI
Passed by Congress July 2, 1909. Ratified February 3, 1913.

The Congress shall have power to lay and collect taxes on incomes, from whatever source derived, without apportionment among the several states, and without regard to any census of enumeration.

Amendment XVII
Passed by Congress May 13, 1912. Ratified April 8, 1913.

The Senate of the United States shall be composed of two Senators from each state, elected by the people thereof, for six years; and each Senator shall have one vote. The electors in each state shall have the qualifications requisite for electors of the most numerous branch of the state legislatures. When vacancies happen in the representation of any state in the Senate, the executive authority of such state shall issue writs of election to fill such vacancies: Provided, that the legislature of any state may empower the executive thereof to make temporary appointments until the people fill the vacancies by election as the legislature may direct. This amendment shall not be so construed as to affect the election or term of any Senator chosen before it becomes valid as part of the Constitution.

Amendment XVIII
Passed by Congress December 18, 1917. Ratified January 16, 1919. Repealed by the 21st Amendment, December 5, 1933.

Section 1.
After one year from the ratification of this article the manufacture, sale, or transportation of intoxicating liquors within, the importation thereof into, or the exportation thereof from the United States and all territory subject to the jurisdiction thereof for beverage purposes is hereby prohibited.

Section 2.
The Congress and the several states shall have concurrent power to enforce this article by appropriate legislation.

Section 3.
This article shall be inoperative unless it shall have been ratified as an amendment to the Constitution by the legislatures of the several states, as provided in the Constitution, within seven years from the date of the submission hereof to the states by the Congress.

Amendment XIX
Passed by Congress June 4, 1919. Ratified August 18, 1920.

The right of citizens of the United States to vote shall not be denied or abridged by the United States or by any state on account of sex. Congress shall have power to enforce this article by appropriate legislation.

Amendment XX
Passed by Congress March 2, 1932. Ratified January 23, 1933.

Section 1.
The terms of the President and Vice President shall end at noon on the 20th day of January, and the terms of Senators and Representatives

at noon on the 3rd day of January, of the years in which such terms would have ended if this article had not been ratified; and the terms of their successors shall then begin.

Section 2.

The Congress shall assemble at least once in every year, and such meeting shall begin at noon on the 3rd day of January, unless they shall by law appoint a different day.

Section 3.

If, at the time fixed for the beginning of the term of the President, the President elect shall have died, the Vice President elect shall become President. If a President shall not have been chosen before the time fixed for the beginning of his term, or if the President elect shall have failed to qualify, then the Vice President elect shall act as President until a President shall have qualified; and the Congress may by law provide for the case wherein neither a President elect nor a Vice President elect shall have qualified, declaring who shall then act as President, or the manner in which one who is to act shall be selected, and such person shall act accordingly until a President or Vice President shall have qualified.

Section 4.

The Congress may by law provide for the case of the death of any of the persons from whom the House of Representatives may choose a President whenever the right of choice shall have devolved upon them, and for the case of the death of any of the persons from whom the Senate may choose a Vice President whenever the right of choice shall have devolved upon them.

Section 5.

Sections 1 and 2 shall take effect on the 15th day of October following the ratification of this article.

Section 6.
This article shall be inoperative unless it shall have been ratified as an amendment to the Constitution by the legislatures of three fourths of the several states within seven years from the date of its submission.

Amendment XXI
Passed by Congress February 20, 1933. Ratified December 5, 1933.

Section 1.
The eighteenth article of amendment to the Constitution of the United States is hereby repealed.

Section 2.
The transportation or importation into any state, territory, or possession of the United States for delivery or use therein of intoxicating liquors, in violation of the laws thereof, is hereby prohibited.

Section 3.
This article shall be inoperative unless it shall have been ratified as an amendment to the Constitution by conventions in the several states, as provided in the Constitution, within seven years from the date of the submission hereof to the states by the Congress.

Amendment XXII
Passed by Congress March 21, 1947. Ratified February 27, 1951.

Section 1.
No person shall be elected to the office of the President more than twice, and no person who has held the office of President, or acted as President, for more than two years of a term to which some other person was elected President shall be elected to the office of the President more than once. But this article shall not apply to any person holding the office of President when this article was proposed

by the Congress, and shall not prevent any person who may be holding the office of President, or acting as President, during the term within which this article becomes operative from holding the office of President or acting as President during the remainder of such term.

Section 2.

This article shall be inoperative unless it shall have been ratified as an amendment to the Constitution by the legislatures of three fourths of the several states within seven years from the date of its submission to the states by the Congress.

Amendment XXIII

Passed by Congress June 16, 1960. Ratified March 29, 1961.

Section 1.

The District constituting the seat of government of the United States shall appoint in such manner as the Congress may direct: A number of electors of President and Vice President equal to the whole number of Senators and Representatives in Congress to which the District would be entitled if it were a state, but in no event more than the least populous state; they shall be in addition to those appointed by the states, but they shall be considered, for the purposes of the election of President and Vice President, to be electors appointed by a state; and they shall meet in the District and perform such duties as provided by the twelfth article of amendment.

Section 2.

The Congress shall have power to enforce this article by appropriate legislation.

Amendment XXIV
Passed by Congress August 27, 1962. Ratified January 23, 1964.

Section 1.
The right of citizens of the United States to vote in any primary or other election for President or Vice President, for electors for President or Vice President, or for Senator or Representative in Congress, shall not be denied or abridged by the United States or any state by reason of failure to pay any poll tax or other tax.

Section 2.
The Congress shall have power to enforce this article by appropriate legislation.

Amendment XXV
Passed by Congress July 6, 1965. Ratified February 10, 1967.

Section 1.
In case of the removal of the President from office or of his death or resignation, the Vice President shall become President.

Section 2.
Whenever there is a vacancy in the office of the Vice President, the President shall nominate a Vice President who shall take office upon confirmation by a majority vote of both Houses of Congress.

Section 3.
Whenever the President transmits to the President pro tempore of the Senate and the Speaker of the House of Representatives his written declaration that he is unable to discharge the powers and duties of his office, and until he transmits to them a written declaration to the contrary, such powers and duties shall be discharged by the Vice President as Acting President.

Section 4.

Whenever the Vice President and a majority of either the principal officers of the executive departments or of such other body as Congress may by law provide, transmit to the President pro tempore of the Senate and the Speaker of the House of Representatives their written declaration that the President is unable to discharge the powers and duties of his office, the Vice President shall immediately assume the powers and duties of the office as Acting President. Thereafter, when the President transmits to the President pro tempore of the Senate and the Speaker of the House of Representatives his written declaration that no inability exists, he shall resume the powers and duties of his office unless the Vice President and a majority of either the principal officers of the executive department or of such other body as Congress may by law provide, transmit within four days to the President pro tempore of the Senate and the Speaker of the House of Representatives their written declaration that the President is unable to discharge the powers and duties of his office. Thereupon Congress shall decide the issue, assembling within forty-eight hours for that purpose if not in session. If the Congress, within twenty-one days after receipt of the latter written declaration, or, if Congress is not in session, within twenty-one days after Congress is required to assemble, determines by two-thirds vote of both Houses that the President is unable to discharge the powers and duties of his office, the Vice President shall continue to discharge the same as Acting President; otherwise, the President shall resume the powers and duties of his office.

Amendment XXVI

Passed by Congress March 23, 1971. Ratified July 1, 1971.

Section 1.

The right of citizens of the United States, who are 18 years of age or older, to vote, shall not be denied or abridged by the United States or any state on account of age.

THE CONSTITUTION OF THE UNITED STATES OF AMERICA

Section 2.
The Congress shall have the power to enforce this article by appropriate legislation.

Amendment XXVII
Originally proposed Sept. 25, 1789. Ratified May 7, 1992.
No law varying the compensation for the services of the Senators and Representatives shall take effect until an election of Representatives shall have intervened.

CHAPTER 7

Socialism, Communism, and Leftism In America

IN PREVIOUS CHAPTERS, we have talked about Socialism in general terms, but I did not go into specifics. Nevertheless, we do know that Socialism and unions have had a long and cozy relationship. We also know that Socialism was being infused into our education system farther back than the 1850s and Socialism heavily migrated toward the Democratic Party. In this chapter, we will look at different types of Socialism, how it moved into our government and other institutions, and how it contributed to the demise of the form of government we had known since 1776.

Socialism comes in many forms and degrees of radicalism. It is worldwide, but we are concerned with that which went on and is still going on in the United States. You must keep in mind the degrees of difference between the names used by or given to the brands of Socialism by the academic community, mainstream media, and society in general. Another point to remember is that regardless of the differences, all are for either demolishing or drastically altering our Constitutional form of government with its capitalistic, free enterprise system. The following will add to the foregoing and will be expanded later in this chapter:

- Leftism: About 10 degrees less harsh than Socialism (depending upon type).
- Socialism: About 10 degrees less harsh than Communism (depending upon type).
- Communism: About 10 degrees more harsh than Socialism (depending upon type).

From the foregoing and information coming later, we can easily say that Leftists, Socialists, and Communists are cousins who support each other in "bringing down" the United States. In the last chapter of this book, we will see how and what we must do to return the United States to it proper position, that being the strongest, most productive and respected country in the world.

As we begin looking at a few of the many types of Socialism, I have found that any and every type failed. I challenge any academic professor or politician to prove differently.

THE NATIONAL SOCIALIST GERMAN WORKERS PARTY (NAZI):

One of the most well-known of the failed Socialist Parties. As we have already seen, Socialism is often a matter of degrees and numerous economies in the world are very Socialistic such as European countries, most of which are now facing financial difficulties. Having lived in France and Germany, as well as much travel (some recently) through many European countries, I can assure you that socialized medicine such as Obamacare will be a nightmare for American citizens. Most Europeans to whom I have spoken were all of the same opinion that for a minor illness that service was not too bad. For illnesses more severe, needed surgical procedures, and necessary tests, their opinions changes to horrendous. Individuals usually had to wait six to nine months for required tests and a year or more for surgical procedures. Although they were paying a reasonable amount for their insurance (taken out of their salary), practically all of them had, in addition, bought individual insurance policies. By having individual/private insurance, they could get an appointment, tests, or surgical procedures within one to two weeks. We must hope that the Supreme Court rules Obamacare unconstitutional and I will show later what it will cost.

[1] MARXIST SOCIALISM OR LENINISM:

Lenin defined Socialism as the transitional stage between Capitalism and Communism. Leninism is Totalitarian, with no Democracy and all decisions are made by the Communist Party. Lenin saw the Communist Party as an "elite that was committed to ending Capitalism and instituting Socialism in its place and attaining the power by any means possible including revolution."

Lenin's death in 1924 brought about the overthrow of his Marxist-Leninism and the imposition of Stalinism. This form of Communism was violent, Totalitarian, and went against some of Lenin's ideas. Under Stalin, many millions of people were killed for the slightest move against the State. It makes one wonder what final type of Socialism/Communism will prevail in the United States, unless we take our country back in the near future.

"DEMOCRATIC" SOCIALISM:

Democratic Socialism is occasionally referred to as Revisionism and prevailed in Western Europe down to the 1970s and is typified by the British Labor Party. It was inspired by Socialism and closely likened to labor unions that had the real power. The role was for the government to own or nationalize all major industries to include banking and airlines. Since labor unions controlled the government, the thought was that unions should control working conditions and wages for the benefit of workers, regardless of the damage to long-term economic growth.

[2] THE EUROPEAN UNION:

The European Union began to evolve in 1958 with six countries as members but growth was steady and the Maastricht Treaty established the European Union under its current name in 1993. A form of Democratic Socialism within the EU was initially considered successful but eventually led to lower social equality and a downward spiraling economy. Beginning in 2010, many European countries were racked with rioting and social unrest. Governments began to back away from out-of-control entitlements that began bankrupting them, which lead to a world financial crisis because of unrestricted debt. The same pattern started in the United States in 2009 and here in the middle of 2011, the Obama administration has done nothing to counteract the problem.

3 BRITAIN, THE LABOR PARTY AND SOCIALISM:

The British Labor Party borrowed Socialist ideas by going to a program of nationalization allowed under Clause Four of their constitution, but was always fundamentally committed to the British system of parliamentary government. Clause Four was dropped after the election of Tony Blair as Party Leader. As a result, former owners of previously nationalized industries were compensated. However, the nationalization of healthcare to create the National Health System made healthcare free at the point of delivery for everybody. The system remains to the present time.

In the 1980s and before the election of Tony Blair, Conservative Prime Minister Margaret Thatcher returned most of the nationalized industries to the private sector. Public Housing was sold to the residents and these conservative measures were endorsed by the "New Labor Party" of Tony Blair.

4 BARRACK OBAMA AND HIS SOCIALISTIC AND "FACIST LIGHT" POLICIES:

In April of 2010, several economists stated that when Obama took office, federal, state, and local spending accounted for thirty percent of our gross domestic product. Now it is up to thirty-five percent and when Obamacare is fully implemented, it will rise to about forty percent. But taxes are still below thirty percent. The difference is the deficit, now grown to ten percent of our GDP.

◄ ONCE THERE WAS AN AMERICA

If our government is to continue spending forty percent of our GDP, we will soon morph into the European model of a Socialist Democracy. But if we roll the spending back to thirty percent, while holding taxes level, we will retain our free market system.

Anita Dunn, political strategist and former (April-November 2009) White House Communications Director, admitted that one of her favorite political philosophers – one that she turns to most – is Mao Zedong. The Communist Dictator responsible for the starvation, torture, and killing of seventy million Chinese.

Critics of the Obama administration have coined the word "Obamunism" to describe Barrack Obama's Socialist and "fascist light" economic planning policies. Benito Mussolini defined Fascism as the wedding of state and corporate powers. Accordingly, trend forecaster Gerald Celeste babbles Obama's corporate bailout as being "fascist light" in the nature. Obamunism can also allude to Obama's ruinous fiscal policies and reckless monetary policies.

Larry (Lawrence) Summers served as Barrack Obama's National Economic Council until late 2010. George Gerald Riesman, Professor Emeritus of Economics at Pepperdine University and author of *Capitalism: A Treatise on Economics*, wrote that Summers is a "lightweight leftist" who "fails to understand the nature of the most essential feature of Capitalism, namely, private ownership of the means of production and the indispensible role it plays in the standard of living of the average person." Professor Riesman also wrote that Summers is a shallow and ignorant man whose knowledge of economics is minimal and whose evil view qualifies him to be the economic advisor to the President of the United States.

During the third week in June 2011, statistics show that the United States fiscal position is such that we must now borrow forty-three cents on every dollar we spend, yet the Obama administration has not submitted a long overdue (three years) budget and have shown little or no inclination to work with Republican Congressman Ryan who has presented a budget with reasonable proposals for the reduction of government spending.

Referring to Obama's unhappy fate of his near one trillion dollar stimulus failure to produce jobs, syndicated Columnist Charles Kraut Hammer stated, "To be sure, Obama has also been promoting a less amusing remedy for anemic growth and high unemployment: exports. In the year's State of the Union address, he proclaimed a national goal of doubling exports by 2014."

One obvious way to increase exports is through free-trade agreements. But unions do not like them. No surprise then that for two years Obama has been sitting on three free-trade agreements with Colombia, Panama, and South Korea – already negotiated by his predecessor.

5 To further show that Socialism/Communism is a failure wherever implemented, we will quickly look at a few other countries.

CUBA:

Communist leader Fidel Castro violently overthrew the Cuban Government in 1950 and has declared Cuba to be a Communist government since then. For several decades, Cuba has faced an overflow of economic problems and the people lack fundamental rights. This once gem of the Caribbean is now a run down, third-world country with no hope for a brighter future. There was some hope Raul (Brother of Fidel) Castro would be able to change the country, but to date he continues to operate in the same manners as Fidel.

NORTH KOREA:

North Korea's form of Communism is in the form of "Juke," a doctrine established by Kim Sung III and carried on by Kim Jong II. The North Korean Government is investing in nuclear weapons and long range missiles to the extent the population is near starvation. Predictions for the current (2011) food crops are dismal and possible severe starvation is within a few months.

VENEZUELA:

The Socialist politics of president-for-life Hugo Chavez (friend of

Obama) have destroyed the economy of this oil rich nation. In 2009, he seized the Venezuelan operations of U.S. based Cargill in order to tighten his grip on the shrinking food supply.

Caracas was once a beautiful and prosperous city. The last time I was there it was shocking and appalling to see the streets patrolled by police and soldiers carrying AK-47s and other automatic weapons. Worse yet, was to see outside the city proper where the thousands upon thousands of people were living in shacks made of scrap wood, tin, and cardboard boxes. I can honestly say it was as bad, if not worse, than the squalid villages I saw in Viet Nam from 1969-1970.

SIMILARITIES BETWEEN COMMUNISM, NAZISM, AND LIBERALISM:

[6] COMMUNIST MANIFESTO	NAZI PARTY PLATFORM	ANALYSIS
"Abolition of property in land application of all rents of land to Public purposes."	We demand an agrarian reform in accordance with our national requirements, and the enactment of a law to expropriate the owners without compensation of any land needed for the common purpose. The abolition of ground rents, andthe prohibition of all speculationin land."	The stripping away of land from private owners. Liberalism today "eminent domain" on property.
"A heavy progressive or graduated income tax."	"We demand the nationalization of trusts – profit-sharing in large Industries – a generous increase old-age pensions – by providing maternity welfare centers, by prohibiting juvenile labor – and the creation of a nation (folk) army."	The points raised in the Nazi platform demand an increase in taxes to support them. Liberalism today demands a heavy progressive and graduated income tax.

SOCIALISM, COMMUNISM, AND LEFTISM IN AMERICA

"Abolition of all rights of inheritance."	"That all unearned income, and all income that does not arise from work, be abolished."	Liberalism today demands a "death tax" on anyone inheriting and estate.
"Confiscation of the property of all emigrants and rebels."	"We demand that all non-Germans who have entered Germany since August 2, 1914 shall be compelled to leave the Reich immediately."	The Nuremberg Laws of 1934 allowed Germany to take Jewish property.
"Centralization of credit in the hands of the state by means of a national bank with State capitol and an exclusive monopoly."	"We demand the nationalization of all trusts."	Central control of the financial system.
"Centralization of the means of communication and transport in the hands of the State."	"We demand that there be a legal campaign against those who propagate deliberate political lies and disseminate them through the press – editors and their assistants on newspapers published in the German language shall be German citizens – Non-German newspapers shall only be published with the express permission of the State – The punishment for transgressing this law the immediate suppression of the newspaper."	Central control of the press. Liberals today demand control or suppression of talk radio and Fox News.

◄ ONCE THERE WAS AN AMERICA

"Free education for all children in public schools. Abolition of children's factory labor in it present form. Combination of Education with industrial with industrial productions, etc."	"In order to make it possible for every capable and industrious German to obtain higher education, and thus the opportunity to reach into positions of leadership, the State must assume the responsibility of organizing thoroughly the entire cultural system of the people. The curricula of all educational establishments shall be adapted to practical life. The conception of the State idea (Science of citizenship) must be taught in the schools from the very beginning. We demand that specially talented children of poor parents whatever their station or occupation, be educated at the expense of the State."	Central control of education with emphasis on doing things their way. Liberals of today are doing things their way in our schools.

As we learned earlier, the House of Un-American Activities Committee's name was changed in 1969 to the House Committee on Internal Security. In 1975, the House abolished the Committee and transferred its functions to the House Judiciary Committee. This was a horrible mistake that was allowed to happen by politicians who were either a part of this cabal, ignorant of what it meant, or as most politicians of that time to the present, they could care less.

As a result of the duties being transferred to the House Judiciary Committee, we had a huge rise in Socialists within our Federal Government. Also, since the time of transfer, the growth of Socialism, Communism, Leftism and other radical groups have grown abundantly in both the government and the general population.

There are several reasons for the foregoing movement. I will use only one example but to many it will be a real eye-opener since it will

SOCIALISM, COMMUNISM, AND LEFTISM IN AMERICA

show you the huge number of Socialists in the 111th Congress. Those names and numbers will change with the takeover of the House of Representatives by the Republican Party for the 112th Congress. I do not have a complete list of the 112th Congress, but I do have the names of some Socialist members who kept their seats.

[7] The Socialist Party of America announced in their October 2009 newsletter that seventy Congressional Democrats currently belong to their caucus. These same seventy United States Congress members are also members of the Democratic Socialists of America (DSA).

[8] The DSA is a political action committee and bills itself as the heir to the defunct Socialist Party of America. Its chief organizing objective is to work within the Democratic Party as the primary, but not the sole method of achieving public ownership of private property.

"Stress our Democratic Party strategy and electoral work. Explain our internal organizing document obtained by World Net Daily. The Democratic Party is something the public understands, and association with it takes the edge off. Stressing our Democratic Party work will establish some distance from the radical subculture and help integrate you to the milieu of the young liberals."

The eleven members of the Democratic Socialist Party of America are/were also members of the House Judiciary Committee. They will also be listed in the complete list of DSA members in the 111th Congress.

John Conyers (Chairman of the Judiciary Committee), Tammy Baldwin, Jerrold Nader, Luis Gutierrez, Maxine Waters, Melvin Watt, Hank Johnson, Steve Cohen, Barbara Lee, Robert Wexler, and Linda Sanchez (there are twenty-three Democrats on the Judiciary Committee, so the above eleven members are practically half of the Committee).

Seventy members of Congress who belong to the caucus of The Socialist Party of America that are also listed as members of The Democratic Socialists of America:

SENATE MEMBERS:

◄ ONCE THERE WAS AN AMERICA

Bernie Sanders – Vermont

HOUSE MEMBERS:
Neil Abercrombie – Hawaii
Tammy Baldwin – Wisconsin
Xavier Bezerra – California
Madeleine Bordello – Guam – At large
Robert Brady – Pennsylvania
Corrine Brown – Florida
Michael Capuano – Massachusetts
Andre Carson – Indiana
Donna Christensen – Virgin Islands – At large
Yvette Clarke – New York
William Lacy Clay – Missouri
Emanuel Cleaver – Missouri
Steve Cohen – Tennessee
John Conyers – Michigan
Elijah Cummings – Maryland
Danny Davis – Illinois
Peter DeFazio – Oregon
Rosa DeLauro – Connecticut
Donna F. Edwards – Maryland
Keith Ellison – Minnesota
Sam Farr – California
Chaka Fatah – Pennsylvania
Bob Filner – California
Barney Frank – Massachusetts
Marcia L. Fudge – Ohio
Alan Grayson – Florida
Luis Gutierrez – Illinois
John Hall – New York
Phil Hare – Illinois
Maurice Hinchey – New York
Michael Honda – California

Jesse Jackson, Jr. – Illinois
Eddie Bernice Johnson – Texas
Hank Johnson – Georgia
Marcy Kaptur – Ohio
Carolyn Kilpatrick – Michigan
Barbara Lee – California
John Lewis – Georgia
David Loeback – Iowa
Ben R. Lucan – New Mexico
Mari Donald Payne – New Jersey
Lyn Maloney – New York
Ed Markey – Massachusetts
Jim McDermott – Washington
James McGovern – Massachusetts
George Miller – California
Gwen Moore – Wisconsin
Jerrold Nader – New York
Eleanor Holmes-Norton – District of Colombia – At large
John Oliver – Massachusetts
Ed Pastor – Arizona
Donald Payne – New Jersey
Chellie Pingree – Maine
Charles Rangel – New York
Laura Richardson – California
Lucille Royal-Mallard – California
Bobby Rush – Illinois
Linda Sanchez – California
Jan Schakowsky – Illinois
Jose Serrano – New York
Louise Slaughter – New York
Pete Stark – California
Bennie Thompson – Mississippi
Jim Tierney – Massachusetts
Nydia Velazquez – New York

Maxine Waters – California
Mel Watt – North Carolina
Henry Waxman – California
Peter Welch – Vermont – At large
Robert Wexler – Florida

[9] THE CONGRESSIONAL PROGRESSIVE CAUCUS:

The Congressional Progressive Caucus is the largest caucus within the Democratic Caucus in the United State Congress. It has eighty-three declared members, and works to advance "progressive" causes. We now know what progressive means so it is no surprise that their objectives include, but not limited to, a more progressive tax system which places a larger portion of corporations and higher income individuals. They want substantial cuts in military spending and more federal programs for social welfare programs at all levels of society.

As you read the list you will notice many members who are also on the list of seventy Democratic Socialists of America Party members who are in Congress.

The Congressional Progressive Caucus list are all members of the Democratic Party. All are declared "progressives" and include all voting Representatives, two non-voting Delegates and one Senator.

[9]NON-VOTING:
Donna Christensen – Virgin Islands
Eleanor Holmes Norton – District of Colombia
SENATE MEMBERS:
Bernie Sanders – Vermont

VOTING REPRESENTATIVES:
Ed Pastor – Arizona
Raul Grijalva – Arizona
Lynn Woolsey – California
George Miller – California
Barbara Lee – California

SOCIALISM, COMMUNISM, AND LEFTISM IN AMERICA

Pete Starke – California
Michael Honda – California
Sam Farr – California
Henry Waxman – California
Judy Chu – California
Karen Bass – California
Lucille Royal-Mallard – California
Marine Water – California
Laura Richardson – California
Linda Sanchez – California
Bob Filner – California
Jared Polis – Colorado
Rose DeLauro – Connecticut
Corrine Brown – Florida
Frederica Wilson – Florida
Alcee Hastings – Florida
Hank Johnson – Georgia
John Lewis – Georgia
Mazie Hirono – Hawaii
Bobby Rush – Hawaii
Jesse Jackson, Jr. – Illinois
Luis Gutierrez – Illinois
Danny Davis – Illinois
Jan Schakowsky – Illinois
Andre Carson – Indiana
David Loeback – Iowa
Chellie Pingree – Maine
Donna Edwards – Maryland
Elijah Cummings – Maryland
John Alver – Massachusetts
Jim McGovern – Massachusetts
Barney Frank – Massachusetts
John Tierney – Massachusetts
Ed Markey – Massachusetts

ONCE THERE WAS AN AMERICA

Mike Capuano – Massachusetts
John Conyers – Michigan
Keith Ellison – Minnesota
Bennie Thompson – Mississippi
William Lacy Clay – Missouri
Emanuel Cleaver – Missouri
Frank Pallone – New Jersey
Donald Payne – New Jersey
Ben R. Lucan – New Mexico
Jerry Nader – New York
Yvette Clarke – New York
Nydia Velazquez – New York
Carolyn Maloney – New York
Charles Rangel – New York
Jose Serrano – New York
Maurice Hinchey – New York
Louise Slaughter – New York
Mel Watt – North Carolina
Mary Kapur – Ohio
Dennis Kucinich – Ohio
Marcia Fudge – Ohio
Peter DeFazio – Pennsylvania
Bob Brady – Pennsylvania
Chaka Fatah – Pennsylvania
Earl Blumenauer – Oregon
Steve Cohen – Tennessee
Sheila Jackson-Lee – Texas
Eddie Bernice Johnson – Texas
Peter Welch – Vermont – At large
Jim Morgan – Virginia
Jim McDermott – Washington
Tammy Baldwin – Wisconsin
Gwen Moore – Wisconsin

SOCIALISM, COMMUNISM, AND LEFTISM IN AMERICA

¹⁰ LEFTIST PARTIES AND ORGANIZATIONS OF NOTE:

As you are probably aware, there are actually thousands (some say only about eleven thousand) Leftist organizations in the United States who would like to see our government overthrown or drastically altered. These groups run freely and the Federal Government simply ignores them. On the other hand, the relatively small right wing groups are under heavy scrutiny and often broken up despite their primary patriotic views.

Although I had considerable knowledge of many subversive groups, I was surprised to find the following list while doing research for his book. I was also surprised that I had no previous knowledge of most of them.

NAME:	IDEOLOGY:
African People's Socialist Party	Black radicalism/nationalism
Anarchist People of Color	Anarchism
Black Radical Congress	Left black radicalism/nationalism
Bring the Ruckus	Anarchist Communism
Freedom Road Socialist Organization/ Arsanijacion Socialists del Camio Para Libertad	Post-Maoism
Freedom Socialist Party	Trotskyism, Socialism, Feminism, radical immigration
Industrial Workers of the World	Revolutionary syndicalism
Northeastern Federation of Anarchists, Communists	American Communism
Party for Socialism and Liberation	Revolutionary Socialism
Peace and Freedom Party	Democratic Socialism
Socialist Party U.S.A	Democratic Socialism

ONCE THERE WAS AN AMERICA

Socialist Workers Party	Post-Trotskyist Castroism
Solidarity	Post-Trotskyist Castroism
Workers International League	Trotskyism
Union del Barrio	Leftism
Workers World Party	Revolutionary

As we leave this chapter on Socialism, Communism, and Leftism, I again remind you that this is another tentacle of the International Bankers (The Evil Octopus) scheme for total world control. They are not concerned with these radical organizations since they can kill them off very quickly, but allow them to operate as a distraction until they reach their final goal.

CHAPTER 8

Socialism In The United States Education System

There have been a certain amount of Socialism surreptitiously injected into our education system that began long before our independence from England. I again remind you of the huge influx of radical university professors who immigrated to the United States during the nineteenth and twentieth centuries when America's immigration doors were wide open. These radical educators were and still are primarily from the field of behavioral science. You will also recall that a large portion of these radical professors were recruited by special interest groups in America and upon arrival were strategically placed in colleges and universities, especially in Eastern schools. These radicals were not immediately cut loose to spread their venom. Instead, they practiced Fabian or "creeping" Socialism for many years.

Although they had to proceed slowly, most of the early radical educators put on their false American faces, became Associate or Full Professors and some eventually became University or College Presidents. Throughout the process, each of these radicals were converting a very good number of future educators to their Socialist philosophy.

The following example relates to the nineteenth and early

twentieth centuries and is intended to show the rapid spread (ripple) effect that three radical professors had on our education system:

UNIVERSITY	PROFESSOR	CONVERTS PER YEAR	TOTAL
H	A	24	
Y	B	21	
P	C	19	64

    Of the foregoing converted future educators, approximately twenty percent would be kept at the respective university for advanced degrees, after which time they would be appointed to the faculty and within eighteen to twenty-four months would be producing a like number of converts to Socialism.

    Approximately forty percent would be sent to other universities for the same pattern of advancement and within the same time period would begin producing converts into the nation's education system.

    The remaining forty percent would immediately begin teaching in the public school system at the secondary level. Nevertheless, they would soft pedal their Socialist views to these younger students. These teachers would be assisted in obtaining advanced degrees during summer studies or leaves of absence. This was necessary in order for them to progress to the level of high school principles or board of education directors. In each case, they would have a great deal of influence upon curriculum and text book selection. One of the prime objectives of properly utilizing new converts was to get them tenure as soon as possible. This pertained to every level of education in which they were teaching. We will discuss tenure later in this chapter.

    As you see by this mushroom effect, three Socialist professors at three liberal universities easily produced thousands of Socialist educators into our education system over a period of several year. I leave this math up to you. Try it, you will be amazed.

    Because of the foregoing, at the present time practically every

SOCIALISM IN THE UNITED STATES EDUCATION SYSTEM

university and college has a faculty overloaded with Socialist or Socialist-leaning professors. This same principle is now down to our lower school levels, to include pre-kindergarten. The sad part of the story is that college graduates of the past thirty-five years do not realize that they have been brainwashed and are teaching the same destructive philosophy to their students.

Naturally, many student educators saw through the scheme and did not accept the "crap" that was spewed upon them. Other educators went to colleges (usually private) who scorned the Anti-American Socialist teachings. Much to their chagrin, these educators are faced with a veiled and often hostile environment whether they are teaching in secondary education or at the college level. They are often openly harassed into changing their mode of teaching in order to conform to the Socialist-leaning of other faculty members and school administrators. Failure to comply usually results in poor performance evaluations, warnings or reprimands, or fabricated deviations of school policy. Harassment continues until the educator acquiesces or is forced to resign.

The following study fits nicely into the example we have used to show the spread of Socialism in our education system from the nineteenth century to the present time. I think you will find the facts very interesting. However, you must remember that, like radical union leaders, radical educators merged with the Democratic Party for a safe haven.

[1] The vastly disproportionate presence of Leftist professors on university campuses across the United States has been well-documented. One of the more significant studies on this subject was done in 2003 by the Center for the Study of Popular Culture which examined the ratio of registered Democrats to registered Republicans on the faculties of thirty-two elite colleges and universities nationwide. These institutions included the entire Ivy League, premier liberal arts colleges like Amherst and Pomona, well-know technical-oriented universities like MIT, highly competitive public institutions such as UC Berkeley and elite universities like Stanford.

◄ ONCE THERE WAS AN AMERICA

The study covered tenured professors in the main areas of study such as economics, political science, etc. We will look into some interesting facts about tenured educators a bit later in this chapter.

In its examination of more than one hundred and fifty departments and upper-level administrators of the thirty-two elite colleges and universities, the Center for the Study of Popular Culture found the overall ratio of registered Democrats and registered Republicans was more than ten to one (eleven thousand three hundred and ninety-seven Democrats, one hundred and thirty-four Republicans).

In the general population of the United States, the number of registered Democrats and Republicans are roughly equal in numbers with a slight edge to the Democrats. But not a single department in any of the thirty-two schools managed to achieve anything remotely approaching parity. The closest found was Northwestern University where eighty percent of the faculty were registered Democrats and only twenty percent were registered Republicans.

At other schools, the ratio of faculty Democrats to Republicans were as follows:

Brown University	30-1
Bowdoin College	23-1
Wellesley College	23-1
Swathmore College	21-1
Amherst College	18-1
Bates College	18-1
Columbia University	14-1
Yale University	14-1
University of Pennsylvania	12-1
Tufts University	12-1
UCLA	12-1
UC Berkeley	12-1
Smith College	11-1

At four schools researchers could not identify a single Republican

◄ 120

on the faculty:

Williams College	51 Democrats	0 Republicans
Oberlin	19 Democrats	0 Republicans
MIT	17 Democrats	0 Republicans
Haverford College	15 Democrats	0 Republicans

The study also found that administrators leaned as far to the left as did the faculties. At schools like the University of Pennsylvania, Carnegie Mellon and Cornell, not a single Republican administrator could be found. Additionally, the study found that no distinction could be made as to Leftist professors in departments whether they were technical or liberal arts.

These figures suggest that most students at these schools graduate without every taking a class taught by a professor with a conservative viewpoint.

Another interesting study conducted by the Foundation for Individual Rights in Education found that more than ninety percent of well-known college campuses have instituted speech codes intended to ban and punish politically incorrect (almost always conservative) speech.

As stated earlier, it is essential to the Socialist take-over of America's education system, that radical educators attain tenure as soon as possible. Once tenure is attained, it is nearly impossible to discharge a radical educator from the system. Once in the ivory towers of tenured academia, the radical educator is protected, not only by the institution, but by the other radicals who are tenured. As a result, he or she has total freedom to propagandize students to any "far out" philosophy that downgrades the United States of America and can publically espouse any Anti-American speech he or she may choose.

The radical tenured educator does the most harm within the halls of academia. He or she joins forces with others of their ilk and block the hire of a new faculty member, assist in blocking tenure of those

◄ ONCE THERE WAS AN AMERICA

who do not share their Leftist views, and strongly influence student newspapers toward "blacklisting" certain students and assuring the newspaper operates with a Leftist agenda. With support from their brothers in crime, they write textbooks that are often accepted and used at some level in our educational system. The following is a good example of how vicious these tenured radical educators can be.

[2] At Duke University in the mid-90s, an American History professor who served in the Army in Viet Nam assumed that his academic career was solid until a group, The Agitprop, started to deny him tenure.

Radical professors set out to destroy him with innuendos, whispered that he was a chauvinist, a racist, a homophobe, and an imperialist – the codeword that strikes fear in university administrators. There was no proof that he deserved any of the labels, but that damage to his reputation became permanent as the drums grew louder. The professor picked up on the slander and decided to accept a position offered from the University of Kentucky to remove himself from the machinations of the Duke scheme.

Undeterred, the radical scholar intensified and transferred their campaign to Kentucky. With anonymous phone calls and unsigned letters, they mobilized their comrades in the Bluegrass State to vilify the professor. The president of the University of Kentucky capitulated, and the job offer was withdrawn. The professor finally found a position at West Point.

When radical scholars run off colleagues, they do not like it because it advances their cause, but even more effective is the campaign to block political heretics from entering the teaching ranks at all. This happened to a Harvard history genius who earned his PhD at U.K.'s Cambridge University (where, by the way, there is no tenure), making him imminently qualified with enviable credentials. He applied to Georgetown and the Air Force Academy for an entrance level chin job, only to be told that he "just wouldn't fit in" – the euphemism adopted by the radical scholars that actually means that "you are not one of us." He now teaches at Marine University and two schools lost

SOCIALISM IN THE UNITED STATES EDUCATION SYSTEM

the services of one of the country's top military scholars.

We have discussed Socialism in our schools to a considerable extent but we have not questioned it. For an answer, we have to go back to earlier discussions wherein it was pointed out that from the beginning the International Bankers (The Illuminati/The Evil Octopus) knew that control of the United States had to be done very gradually and as conditions permitted. They were very astute and worked in various ways, but Socialism had to be well-established.

After being established, the first and most important target was education. The Socialists were tactful and did not proclaim themselves as Socialists. Instead, they used more acceptable words like "progressive" (recently started being used again), "liberal," "moderate," etc. as a means of deceiving. Although this will be discussed in depth later, American citizens, especially parents were and are just too unconcerned, busy, and lethargic to focus on what really goes on in our academic institutions. Likewise, our politicians are even more guilty of our downfall since they probably know what is happening but do not have the necessary character to stop the movement. They know the power of the academic community and will do almost anything to get and keep their votes.

[3] Norman Thomas, a Socialist member of the American Civil Liberties Union, boldly told the world: "The American people will never knowingly adopt Socialism, but under the name of Liberalism will accept every fragment of the Socialist program until one day America will be a Socialist nation without even knowing how it happened."

[4] In 1936, the National Education Association (more later) stated the position from which it has never wavered: "We stand for socializing the individual." The NEA, and its Policy for American Education opined, "The major problem of education in our times arises out of fact that we live in a period of fundamental social change. In the new democracy (Note: we are not a democracy, we are a constitutional republic), education must share in the responsibility of giving purpose and direction to social change. The major function of the school is the

social orientation of the individual – Education must operate according to a well-formulated social policy."

[5] Chester M. Pierce, M.D., Professor of Education and Psychiatry at Harvard, had this to say: "Every child in America entering school at the age of five is mentally ill because he comes to school with certain allegiances to our Founding Fathers, toward elected officials, toward his parents, toward a belief in a supernatural being, and toward the sovereignty of the nation as a separate entity. It is up to you as teachers to make all these sick children well – by creating the international child of the future."

[6] Victor Gollancz, a famous Socialist publisher, explained why he believes that Socialism will take over America: "Christians are not exactly bright, so it will be easy for Socialists to lead them down the garden path through their ideas of brotherly love and social justice."

Now that I have already mentioned it, we will take a closer look at the National Education Association and the American Federation of Teachers. Both are Liberal, Leftist, Socialist, and radical organizations who control our schools and influence our children from pre-kindergarten to doctorate programs. They use their power to select the curriculum, books, teaching methods, and aids. As parents, either through ignorance or lack of concern, we turn our children over to these demons to be molded into something we did not intend.

There are differences between these two powerful unions of which we need to be aware. [7] The National Education Association with three-point-two million members in most likely the most powerful union in the United States. It was founded in 1857 and anyone working for a public school district, college, university, or any other public institution devoted to education is eligible to join. The National Education Association's membership is more concentrated in suburban or rural areas in the West. The American Federation of Teachers was formed in 1916, and has one-point-five members (2010) who tend to be in large cities and on the East Coast. The

SOCIALISM IN THE UNITED STATES EDUCATION SYSTEM ➤

Union represents higher education faculty (including professors, non-tenure-track faculty, and graduate student employees), nurses working in private-sector hospitals, state public employees, school nurses, schools librarians, and educational Para-professionals, such as drivers and cafeteria workers.

The National Education Association describes itself as a professional employee organization, is incorporated as such in a few states and as a labor union in most states. All of this is simply window-dressing, since from its early years it has been a radical Leftist organization whose main purpose was and is to socialize America by teaching our children to ignore traditional family, religious and patriotic values. In their place, children were and are taught far left philosophies that include bringing about the downfall of our constitutional form of government and becoming part of a New World Order/One-World Government. Naturally, they teach that this new order is Socialist, Anti-Christian, and that nothing is absolute and everything is relevant (How absurd can you get?). We should now look at some examples of what the National Education Association really is:

We have already studied that the openly stated position of the National Education Association is: "We stand for socializing the individual." And they openly speak of the education practices they will be using in the "new" democracy (New World Order/One-World Government) so it is no surprise when we read of more radical involvement by the National Education Association.

[9] The National Education Association has made a glowing assessment of radical Socialist community organizer, Saul Alinsky (one of Obama's heroes), and highly recommends American public school children to read two of his books, including one dedicated to Satan.

The NEA recommends Alinsky's "Reveille for Radicals," a 1946 book about the principles and tactics of "community organizing," and "Rules for Radicals," a 1971 text that articulates a Socialist strategy for gaining political power to redistribute wealth from the "haves" to the "have-nots."

Alinksy dedicated the first edition of his book "Rules for Radicals" to Satan: "Lest we forget at least an over-the-shoulder acknowledgement to the very first radical known to man who rebelled against the establishment and did it so effectively that he at least won his own kingdom – Lucifer." We will take a much deeper look at Alinsky in another chapter.

The following article appeared in the January 1946 edition of the National Education Association Journal: "In the struggle to establish an adequate world government, the teachers ... can do much to prepare the hearts and minds of children for global understanding and cooperation ... At the very top of the agencies which will assure the coming of world government must stand the school, the teacher, and the organized profession."

[10] During a working session at the United Nations, National Education Association's representative, Diane Schneider, said that graphic sexual education needs to be taught in the classroom. Also, during a panel discussion on how to best combat homophobia and transphobia, Schneider stated, "oral sex, masturbation, and orgasms need to be taught in the classroom," according to attendee, Austin Rush, who is president of the California Family and Human Rights Institute. Schneider noted that "gender identity expression" and "sexual orientation" are a spectrum and those opposed to homosexuality are stuck "in a binary box that religion and family creates."

In 1979, the National Education Association held its annual Conference on Human and Civil Rights where the radical Jean Houston was the keynote speaker. Houston said that "many teachers have opened the minds of children from darkness to Illuminist humanity (Does this sound familiar?), that moral mandates, religions, and the standard form of governments are breaking down. The New Age is seeded and created and who is it done by? I suggest largely by educators."

[11] The National Education Association has a budget of more than three hundred and seven million dollars for the 2006-2007 fiscal

SOCIALISM IN THE UNITED STATES EDUCATION SYSTEM

year. As you see, the organization with its three-point-two million members is not hurting for money.

The exorbitant dues that teachers pay to the NEA enable its well-paid staff to lobby Congress and state legislatures on behalf of their goals. In its history, the National Education Association has never contributed one dime to conservative candidates running for public office at any level. Conversely, the NEA has contributed many millions of dollars to the Democratic Party.

As stated earlier, the American Federation of Teachers, with one-point-five million members, is much smaller in comparison to the three-point-two million members of the National Education Association. Their membership is more diverse and their labor tactics are different.

[12] "The American Federation of Teachers was founded in the belief that public education and its employees should be based on an industrial labor model." That is, collective bargaining agreements will be negotiated that focus almost exclusively on employee welfare. Pay, benefits, and time-off make up the bulk of the negotiations.

The American Federation of Teachers has been assisted by labor unions and is exceptionally adept in contract negotiations. It often bullies elected and appointed school leaders, contributes dues dollars to radical groups, and puts the interest of its members ahead of students. A former American Federation of Teachers president stated, "When schoolchildren start paying dues, [that is] when [I will] start representing the interest of the schoolchildren."

Like the somewhat more sophisticated National Education Association, the American Federation of Teachers idolize the Socialist/Communist "father of modern education," John Dewey. Also, like the NEA, the AFT recommends that teachers and students read and study the previously mentioned books of the extreme radical, Saul Alinsky.

As you easily see, a steady stream of Anti-American, Socialist/Communist venom has been injected into our schools and the minds of our children for many, many decades. Backed by stacks of valid data, I can confidently estimate that anyone graduating from high school and a four-year college degree program since 1960 has been brainwashed and, unless self-educated after graduation, is ignorant of what brought about the downfall of the United States. This is especially true of those with degrees in education. Sadly and perhaps unknowingly, they have taught a false doctrine and many of their students are now teachers themselves, continuing to promote this Anti-American doctrine.

CHAPTER 9

The Council On Foreign Relations

AS WE BEGIN discussing the Council of Foreign Relations, keep in mind that you are studying another tentacle of The Evil Octopus – The International Bankers/The Illuminati. When writing on this subject, authors may use terms like "The Establishment," "The Insiders," "The Invisible Government," "The Shadow Government," etc. All are synonyms for the Council of Foreign Relations.

The Council on Foreign Relations presents itself as a think tank and states its mission to be: "a resource for its members, government officials, business executives, journalists, educators and students, civic and religious leaders, and other interested citizens in order to help them better understand the world and foreign policy ... choices facing the United States and other countries." This innocuous statement may be true for their public purpose, but we will soon get to the real Council on Foreign Relations as we progress through this chapter.

The Council on Foreign Relations was founded in 1921 by Edward Mendell House, a Marxist advisor and long-time close friend to President Woodrow Wilson. Many historians refer to "Colonel" House as Wilson's "handler." No one knows where his title came from since he was never in the military service. Other historians refer to him as Wilson, alter ego and the most influential and powerful man in America two terms as President. House wrote a novel, published in 1912, entitled "Phillip Drew: Administrator." He later acknowledged the book as his own. In his book, House stated that he was working for "Socialism as dreamed of by Karl Marx." Also in his book, "Colonel" House relayed his plan for conquering the United States. He also explained how both the Democratic and Republican parties would be controlled and used in creating a Socialist government in America and becoming a member of a one-world government.

With a Marxist "handler" in "Colonel" House and a Socialist-leaning President in Woodrow Wilson, it is not surprising that the Federal Reserve System (a private central bank) was created in violation of our Constitution, during the first year of Wilson's Presidency. Also, during this same year, the graduated income tax was ratified. As you probably know, the control of all political parties, a private central bank, and the graduated income tax were all original ideas of Karl Marx.

It is difficult to say whose administration has done the most destruction to our Constitutional Republic. However, if I had been pushed for an answer three years ago it would have been Woodrow Wilson and I still cringe with repulsion when I pass his boyhood home in downtown Augusta, Georgia. With two years and nine months of Barrack Obama, I have changed my mind.

[2] From its beginning in 1921, the Council on Foreign Relations began to attract men of power and influence. In the late 1920s, important financing for the CFR came from the Rockefeller Foundation and the Carnegie Foundation. In 1940, at the invitation of President Franklin D. Roosevelt, members of the Council on Foreign Relations gained domination over the State Department, and they have maintained this control ever since.

Carrel Quigley, Professor of History at Georgetown University, a CFR member and Bill Clinton's mentor wrote in his book "Tragedy and Hope:" "The CFR is the American branch of a society which originated in England, and which believes that national boundaries should be obliterated, and a one-world rule established."

[3] Rear Admiral Chester Ward who was a member of the Council on Foreign Relations for 16 years warned the United States of the

THE COUNCIL ON FOREIGN RELATIONS

organizations intentions: "The most powerful clique in these elitist groups have one objective in common ... they want to bring about the surrender of the sovereignty of the national independence of the United States. A second clique of international members in the CFR comprises the Wall Street International Bankers and their key agents. Primarily, they want the world banking monopoly from whatever power ends up in control of the government."

The Council on Foreign Relations has always attracted top notch, influential members from all relevant areas of our nation such as finance, business, manufacturing, government officials, military leaders, politicians, educators, and the mainstream news media and in essence, controls every aspect of our lives.

[4] The CFR intends to maintain a diverse membership, including special programs to promote interest and develop expertise in the coming generations of foreign policy leaders. The Council on Foreign Relations held meetings at which government officials, One-World leaders, and prominent members of the foreign policy community discuss major international issues. The David Rockefeller Studies Program has approximately one hundred and fifty full-time and adjunct professors. In addition, there are ten in-residence recipients of year-long fellowships who cover the main regions and significant issues shaping today's international (one-world government) agenda. These scholars contribute to the foreign policy debate by making recommendations to the presidential administration, testifying before Congress, serving as a resource to the diplomatic community, interacting with the media, authoring books, reports, and op-eds on foreign policy issues. Most members do not know it but there is an inner circle of members who hold the real power and control of the organization.

As a retired Regular Army officer and a veteran of the Korean War and the View Nam War, it saddens me to relate that in 1962 the [5] Council on Foreign Relations began a program of bringing select military officers to the Harold Pratt House to study along with its scholars. This is not surprising since we have had many key military officers who were/are CFR members for decades. How do you think Dwight D. Eisenhower went from a lower rated Lieutenant Colonel to five-star General in a short period of time and eventually President of the United States? The Commander of all military forces in Viet Nam, General William Westmoreland was a CFR member. A more recent example is a CFR member, General David Petraeus, hero of the War in Iraq and Commander, United States Central Command.

The foregoing ties in with the Yalta Conference in February 1945. This conference is frequently referred to as "The Sell-Out at Yalta." Without going into great detail, our wonderful Socialist President Franklin D. Roosevelt, Prime Minister Winston Churchill of England and Generalissimo Joe Stalin of Russia carved up part of Europe and, in doing so, created the Soviet Bloc which enslaved many nations under Communist rule and killed several million people in the process. This harsh rule continued until President Ronald Reagan forced the downfall of Communist Russia.

A major point concerning the Sell-Out at Yalta needs to be discussed separately. At this conference President Roosevelt and other American leaders laid plans that there could never be military leaders like General George Patton, General Mark Clark, Admiral Chesty Puller, etc. The question arises: why? Roosevelt knew that the move toward a one-world government would result in "no win" wars and we had to have "yes" men as our military leaders. The Council on Foreign Relations and others simply could not have winners conducting wars. We saw the last of the real Generals put away when President Harry Truman relieved General Douglas MacArthur in the early stages of the Korean War. There were a few other issues but General MacArthur simply wanted to win the war by crossing the 38th Parallel and "kicking butt" in North Korea and Chinese if they intervened, which they later did. The Council on Foreign Relations just could not allow this to happen since they had future plans for China.

Without doubt, the Council on Foreign Relations is the most dangerous Anti-American cabal in existence. Most Americans have never heard of it and when introduced to it usually refuse to accept it. This is somewhat understandable since the truth about such matters has not been presented in our schools, churches, and mainstream news media. It is also understandable that uninformed citizens find it hard to believe that such prominent, influential, and highly accomplished individuals could be involved in such a plot against their own country. They forget that this information has been deliberately withheld from the television, newspapers, magazines, and naturally, their formal education. They also forget that America has always had its Benedict Arnold's throughout our history. Looked at with an open mind, the prominent members of the CFR are no better than others who want to destroy our Republic, such as the New Black Panther Party and the Ku Klux Klan.

There are other reasons why the average citizen does not know about the Council on Foreign Relations. It was mainly kept secret for several decades. The first time I heard of it was in the late 1960s and information was then hard to find. Also near that time there were more than one hundred and fifty media executives and reporters who were CFR members and were certainly not going to publicize its existence or workings.

The CFR began to become a bit more open in the late 1980s and today they are much more open. They have their own website, [6] publish their own magazines name "Foreign Affairs" which is considered the preeminent journal of international affairs. It also publishes "Independent Task Force" which brings together experts with diverse backgrounds and expertise to work together to produce reports offering both findings and policy prescriptions on important foreign policy topics. However, whatever is said in meetings is kept secret.

When I first read about the Council on Foreign Relations, probably in 1967, there were approximately one thousand and five hundred members listed. Today the CFR boasts a membership of five thousand or more. This is really scary when you have this many people working in high government positions or others exerting influence toward the destruction of our Constitutional Republic and our future way of life. Always remember that the end game is a one-world government.

◀ ONCE THERE WAS AN AMERICA

They may speak of equality, redistribution of wealth, etc., but it will be a two-class society consisting of the controlling few and the remainder of us as an "amalgamated mess" to be maneuvered around as deemed appropriate.

In closing out this chapter, I am including the most up-to-date listing of CFR members I can find. The list certainly does not include all members. It is fairly recent but you will see some changes like the death of Geraldine Ferraro a few months ago. I am sure you will be amazed to see the names of people who are of the brightest minds and accomplishment in their respective fields. This list does not contain all five thousand members but gives you many notable current members and some past notable members.

I am sure you will agree that there is a small group of members who are not totally committed to carrying out all aspects of this conspiracy. Of this group, many were flattered by the invitation to join such an august "study group." Others become members for prestige, a high profile job, or other personal reasons. However, like all members they are used to promote the destruction of our Republic and free enterprise system.

MEMBERS OF THE COUNCIL ON FOREIGN RELATIONS:

BOARD OF DIRECTORS:
The Board of Directors is composed of thirty-six officers. Peter G. Peterson and David Rockefeller are Directors Emeriti (Chairman Emeritus and Honorary Chairman, respectively). It also has an International Advisory Board consisting of thirty-five distinguished individuals from across the world.

OFFICE	NAME
Co-Chairman of the Board	Carla A. Hills
Co-Chairman of the Board	Robert E. Rubin
Vice Chairman	Richard E. Salomon

THE COUNCIL ON FOREIGN RELATIONS ➤

President	Richard N. Haas

Board of Directors

Former Commander, CENTCOM	John Abizaid
Founder, International Center on Nonviolent Conflict	Peter Ackerman
Professor in Middle East Studies, John Hopkins University	Found Ajami
Former Secretary of State	Madeleine K. Albright
Former President, Northwestern University	Henry S. Bienne
Economics Professor, Princeton University	Alan Blinder
Managing Partner, Boies &McInnis	Mary Boies
Chairman, Atlantic Media Company	David G. Bradley
Former Editor, NBC Nightly News	Tom Brokaw
Bill and Melinda Gates Foundation	Sylvia Matthews Burwell
Former White House Chief-of-Staff	Kenneth M. Duberstein
Economics Professor, Harvard University	Martin Feldstein
Forman Chairman, Foreign Intelligence Advisory Board	Stephen Friedman
Former CEO, Young & Rubicam	Ann M. Fudge
President, Claremont McKenna College	Pamela Gann
Vice Chairman, The Blackstone Group	J. Tomilson Hill
Former U.S. Diplomat	Donna Hrinak
John S. and James L. Knight Foundation	Alberto Ibarguen
President, Rensselaer Polytechnic Institute	Shirley Jackson
Co-Founder, Kohlberg Kravis	

◄ ONCE THERE WAS AN AMERICA

Roberts & Co.	Henry R. Kravis
Former Deputy Director for Intelligence	Jami Miscik
Kennedy School of Government	Joseph S. Nye
Chairman, Caterpillar Inc.	James W. Owens
Chairman, Peter G. Peterson Foundation	Peter G. Peterson
Former Secretary of State & Chief-of-Staff, U.S. Army	Colin L. Powell
CEO, Pritzker Realty	Penny Pritzker
Co-Founder, The Carlyle Group	David M. Rubenstein
President, International Rescue Committee	George Erik Rupp
CEO, FedEx	Frederick W. Smith
Former Ambassador	Joan E. Sperm
CEO, Clark & Weinstock	Vin Weber
Former Governor of New Jersey	Christine Todd
Editor-At-Large, Time Magazine	Fareed Zakaria

NOTABLE CURRENT COUNCIL MEMBERS:

- Madeleine Albright – 64th United States Secretary of State
- Eliot Abrams – International lawyer, diplomat
- John Abizaid – U.S. Army General, former Head of CENTCOM
- John B. Anderson – former Republican/Independent Congressman from Illinois
- Anthony Clark Arendt – International lawyer, and academic
- Howard Baker – 13th Senate Majority Leader of the United States Senate, former Senator from Tennessee, former Chief-of-Staff to Ronald Reagan, husband of Nancy Kassebaum Baker
- James Baker – 61st Secretary of State of the United States, and 67th Secretary of the Treasury of the United States
- Michael D. Barnes – former United States Democrat Congressman from Maryland, and President of the Brady Campaign
- Joe Biden – 47th Vice-President of the United States

THE COUNCIL ON FOREIGN RELATIONS

- Josh Bolton – former Chief-of-Staff to George W. Bush
- Rudy Boschwitz – former Republican United States Senator from Minnesota
- Sandy Berger – United States National Security Advisor under President Bill Clinton
- Michael R. Bloomberg – Current Mayor of New York City
- Bill Brock – former Republican United States Senator from Tennessee
- Erin Burnett – CNBC anchor
- Tom Brokaw – journalist at NBC
- Howard Berman – United States Congressman from California
- Peter Beinart – academic and columnist
- L. Paul Bremer – diplomat
- Edgar Bronfman – member of the Bronfman dynasty, President of the World Jewish Congress
- Ethan Bronner – Deputy Foreign Editor of The New York Times
- Zbigniew Brzezinski – United States National Security Advisor to President Jimmy Carter
- Stephen Gerald Breyer – United States Supreme Court Justice
- Jonathan S. Bush – Healthcare CEO, son of Jonathan Bush, brother of NBC entertainment reporter Billy Bush
- Jimmy Carter – 39th President of the United States
- Frank Carlucci – 16th Secretary of Defense under Ronald Reagan
- Dick Cheney – 46th Vice-President of the United States
- Juju Chang – newsreader on Good Morning America
- Warren Christopher – former United States Secretary of State
- Bill Clinton – 42nd President of the United States
- Hillary Rodham Clinton – 67th United States Secretary of State
- Henry Cisneros – former Secretary of Housing and Urban Development under Bill Clinton
- Mario Cuomo – former Governor of New York
- Michael Crow – President of Arizona State University
- Kate Couric – CBS anchor

◄ ONCE THERE WAS AN AMERICA

- Stephen F. Cohen – Professor of Russian Studies at NYU, husband of Katrina van den Heuvel
- Ed Cox – International attorney, Chairman of the New York Republic Party, son-in-law of Richard Nixon
- Kenneth Duberstein – former Chief-of-Staff to Ronald Reagan
- Peggy Dulany – 4th child of David Rockefeller
- Joseph Duffey – academic and educator
- Chris Dodd – United States Senator from Connecticut
- Michael Dukakis – former Democratic Governor of Massachusetts
- Mervyn M. Dymally – former Democratic Congressman from California
- Lawrence Eaglerberger – former Untied States Secretary of State under President George H. W. Bush
- Karl Eikenerry – United States Army General, Ambassador to Afghanistan
- Roger W. Ferguson, Jr. – former Vice-Chairman of the Federal Reserve
- Noah Feldman – academic and author
- Alan H. Fleischmann – Co-Founder of ImagineNations Group
- Dianne Feinstein – United States Senator from California
- Donald M. Fraser – former Democratic Congressman from Minnesota
- Mikhail Fridman – Russian oligarch, International Advisory Board Member
- Thomas Friedman – journalist, The New York Times
- Geraldine Ferraro – former Democratic Congresswoman from New York
- Tom Foley – 57th speaker of the United States House of Representatives
- Pamela Gann – President of Claremont McKenna College, former Dean of Duke University School of Kaw
- Robert M. Gates – United States Secretary of Defense, former Director of Central Intelligence

THE COUNCIL ON FOREIGN RELATIONS

- Leslie Gelb – former journalist for The New York Times
- Dick Gephardt – 22nd Majority leader of the United States House of Representatives
- Sam Gejdenson – former Democratic Congressman from Connecticut
- Alan Greenspan – former Chairman of the Federal Reserve
- Maurice R. Greenberg – former Chairman and CEO of AIG
- Bob Graham – former Democratic Governor and Senator of Florida
- Janet G. Mullins Grissom – Republican lobbyist, former state department official
- David Gergen – advisor to Richard Nixon, Gerald R. Ford, Ronald Reagan, and Bill Clinton, commentator for CNN
- Mikhail Gorbachev – last President of the USSR
- Roy M. Goodman – former Republican member of the New York State Senate
- Newt Gingrich – 58th Speaker of the United States House of Representatives
- Ruth Bader Ginsburg – United States Supreme Court Justice
- Tenzin Gyatso – 14th Dalai Lama
- Richard N. Haas – former State Department official
- David A. Harris – Director of the American Jewish Committee (AJC)
- Sidney Harman – businessman, owner of Newsweek, husband of Jane Harman
- Lee Hamilton – former Democratic Congressman from Indiana
- Michael Hayden – United States Air Force General, former Director of the National Security Agency and CIA
- Gary Hart – former Democratic U.S. Senator representing Colorado, Council for a Livable World Chairman, advisory board member for the Partnership for a Secure America
- Chris Heinz – Heir to the H.J. Heinz Company ketchup fortune
- Carla Anderson Hills – former Secretary of Housing and Urban Development under Gerald Ford

ONCE THERE WAS AN AMERICA

- Kim Holmes – foreign policy and defense expert
- Douglas Holtz-Eakin – Economist
- Warren Hoge – American journalist, formerly of The New York Times
- Malcolm Hoenlein – Vice-Chairman of the Conference of Presidents of Major American Jewish Organizations
- William van den Heuvel – diplomat and international lawyer
- Katrina van den Heuvel – Editor of The Nation, wife of Stephen F. Cohen
- Frederick Iseman – businessman, inventor
- Angelina Jolie – actress, UN Goodwill Ambassador
- Vernon Jordan – close advisor to President William J. Clinton
- Nancy Johnson – former Republican Congresswoman from Connecticut
- Woody Johnson – investor, owner of the New York Jets, heir to Johnson & Johnson
- Sheila Johnson – businesswoman, President of the Washington Mystics
- Walter H. Kansteiner, III – American diplomat
- Peter J. Katzenstein – Political Scientist, academic
- Thomas Kean, Sr. – former Republican Governor of New Jersey
- Robert Kagan – co-founded Project for the New American Century, husband of Victoria Nuland
- Nancy Kassebaum – former Republican Senator from Kansas, daughter of Alf Landon, and wife of Howard Baker
- John Kerry – United States Senator of Massachusetts
- Henry Kissinger – former United States Secretary of State, former Security Advisor
- Paul R. Krugman – economist, columnist for The New York Times
- Larry Kudlow – economist, radio talk show host, CNBC talk show host
- Charles Krauthammer – columnist, political commentator at Fox News

THE COUNCIL ON FOREIGN RELATIONS

- Zalmay Khalilzad – diplomat, former Ambassador to the United States
- Jim Leach – former Republican Congressman from Iowa, Chairman of the National Endowment for Humanities
- John Robert Lewis – Democratic Congressman from Georgia, Civil Rights leader
- Jim Lehrer – anchor for PBS
- Joe Lieberman – United States Senator from Connecticut
- Lewis Libby – attorney, former Chief-of-staff to Vice-President Dick Cheney
- David Malpass – economist, Republican politician
- John McCain – United States Senator of Arizona
- Bud McFarlane – former National Security Advisor to Ronald Reagan
- George McGovern – former Democratic Senator from South Dakota
- William Green Miller – United States Ambassador to Ukraine under Bill Clinton
- George J. Mitchell – 17th Senate Majority Leader of the United States Senate, former Senator of Maine
- Walter Mondale – 42nd Vice-President of the United States of America
- Bill Moyers – former press-secretary to Lyndon Johnson, public commentator for PBS
- Heather Nauert – journalist and anchor for Fox News
- John D. Negroponte – United States Deputy Secretary of State, former Director of Nation Intelligence, former U.S. Ambassador to Honduras
- Joseph Nye – academic
- Sandra Day O'Connor – former United States Supreme Court Justice
- Stan O'Neal – Chief Executive Officer and Chairman of the Board of Merrill Lynch
- Henry Paulson – United States Treasury Secretary

- David Patraeus – United States Army General, Head of CENTCOM
- Peter G. Peterson – 20th United States Secretary of Commerce
- Kitty Pilgrim – CNN journalist
- Richard Pipes – academic, father of founder/director of Middle East Forum, Daniel Pipes
- Daniel Pipes – academic, writer, historian
- Norman Podhoretz – former Editor-in-Chief of "Commentary," senior fellow at the Hudson Institute, Project or the New American Century (PNAC) signatory
- Steve Poizner – California businessman and Republican politician
- Roman Popadiuk – former United States Ambassador to Ukraine, Executive Director of the George Bush Presidential Library Foundation
- Colin Powell – former United States Secretary of State, former National Security Advisor, former Chairman of the Joint Chiefs of Staff
- Tom Petri – Republican Congressman from Wisconsin
- Charles Prince – Chief Executive officer of Citigroup
- Condoleezza Rice – 66th United States Secretary of State
- Dan Rather – journalist, former anchor of CBS
- Charles Rangel – United States Congressman from New York City
- Keith A. Ridley, IV – Washington, D.C., businessman
- Alice Rivlin – economist, former U.S. Cabinet member
- David Rockefeller, Jr.
- John D. Rockefeller, IV – United States Senator of West Virginia
- Charlie Rose – PBS journalist
- Chuck Robb – former Democratic Governor/Senator of Virginia, son-in-law of Lyndon B. Johnson
- Edward Regan – former State Comptroller of New York
- Robert Rubin – 70th Secretary of the Treasury under Bill Clinton
- Diane Sawyer – anchor for ABC News
- Stephen M. Schwebel – jurist, former judge on the International

THE COUNCIL ON FOREIGN RELATIONS

Court of Justice
- Dan Senor – former foreign policy advisor to George W. Bush, Fox News foreign policy analyst
- Amity Shlaes – Bloomberg News columnist and author
- Timothy Striver – Chairman and CEO of the Special Olympics
- David Stern – Commissioner of the NBA
- John Spratt – former Democratic Congressman from South Carolina
- Jeffrey D. Sachs – American economist
- Karenna Gore Schiff – daughter of Al Gore
- Olympia J. Snowe – Republican Senator from Maine
- Brent Scowcroft – United States National Security Advisor under Presidents Gerald Ford and George H.W. Bush
- George Schultz – former United States Secretary of State, former United States Secretary of the Treasury, former United States Secretary of Labor
- Frederick W. Smith – CEO and Founder of FedEx
- Walter B. Slocombe – former Under Secretary of Defense for Policy
- George Soros – Currency Speculator, investor, and business
- Lesley Stahl – CBS journalist
- Donna Shalala – former Secretary of Health and Human Services under Bill Clinton
- Eduard Shevardnadze – 2nd President of Georgia
- Adlai Stevenson III – former Democratic Senator from Illinois
- George Stephanopoulos – former press secretary under Bill Clinton, co-host of Good Morning America
- Laurence H. Silberman – United States federal judge
- Stansfield Turner – United States Navy Admiral, former head of the CIA
- Richard Thornburgh – 76th Attorney-General of the United States of America under Reagan and Bush
- Fred Thompson – actor, radio talk-show host, former Senator from Tennessee, Presidential candidate

- Shirley Temple – actress, diplomat
- Paul Volcker – former Chairman of the Federal Reserve
- Rick Warren – American Christian leader
- Peter J. Wallison – 20th White House Counsel to Ronald Reagan, former lawyer to Nelson Rockefeller
- Barbara Walters – ABC News journalist
- Vin Weber – former United States Republican Congressman from Minnesota
- Steven Weinberg – American physicist
- John C. Whitehead – Chairman of the World Trade Center Memorial Foundation, former United States Deputy Secretary of State under Ronald Reagan, former Goldman Sachs Chairman
- Christine Todd Whitman – former Republican Governor of New Jersey and Head of the Environmental Protection Agency
- Shirley Williams, Baroness Williams of Crosby – British member of Parliament and International Advisory Board member
- Richard S. Williamson – diplomat, lawyer, and Republican politician
- Adam Wolfensohn
- James D. Wolfensohn – former President of the World Bank
- Paul Wolfowitz – former President of the World Bank and former U.S. Deputy Secretary of Defense
- James Woolsey – former Director of Central Intelligence and former Head of the Central Intelligence Agency
- Paula Zahn – journalist, former anchor at CNN
- James Zogby – academic, political commentator, and pollster
- Robert Zoellick – President of the World Bank

NOTABLE HISTORICAL MEMBERS:
- Kenneth Bacon – American journalist
- Conrad Black – International Advisory Board Member
- George Wildman Ball – American diplomat
- Spruille Braden – American diplomat and businessman

THE COUNCIL ON FOREIGN RELATIONS

- McGeorge Bundy – National Security Advisor for Presidents John F. Kennedy and Lyndon B. Johnson
- William Bundy – CIA agent, historian
- William F. Buckley, Jr. – commentator, publisher, and founder of the National Review
- Paul Cravath – lawyer, one of the Founders of the Council on Foreign Relations
- Monica Crowley – former Richard Nixon aide, radio host, and columnist
- John Chafee – former Secretary of the Navy and Republican Senator from Rhode Island
- Michael Raoul Duval – attorney for Richard Nixon and Gerald Ford
- C. Douglas Dillon – 57th Secretary of the Treasury of the United States under John F. Kennedy and Lyndon Johnson
- Allen Dulles – former Director of the CIA
- John Foster Dulles – 52nd Secretary of State of the United States under Ike Eisenhower
- President Gerald Ford
- Alexander Haig – United States Army General, 59th Secretary of State of the United States under Ronald Reagan
- Armand Hammer – businessman and investor
- W. Averell Harriman – former Democratic Governor of New York, diplomat
- H. John Heinz III – former Republican Senator from Pennsylvania
- Henry Hyde – former Republican Congressman from Illinois
- Sergei Karaganov – International Advisory Board member
- Irving Kristol – journalist, writer, dubbed "The Godfather of Neo-Conservatism," father of Bill Kristol
- George Kennan – diplomat and historian
- Jeane Kirkpatrick – diplomat, former Ambassador to the United Nations
- Robert Lovett – 4th Secretary of Defense of the United States

ONCE THERE WAS AN AMERICA

- John J. McCoy – lawyer and banker
- Charles Peter McColough – businessman
- Robert McNamara – 8th Secretary of Defense, former World Bank President
- Daniel Patrick Moynihan – diplomat, former Democratic Senator from New York
- Edmund Muskie – 58th Secretary of State of the United States
- Richard M. Nixon – 37th President of the United States
- Paul Nitze – Secretary of the Navy under Lyndon Johnson
- Nelson Rockefeller – 41st Vice-President of the United States and Governor of New York
- John D. Rockefeller, III
- Felix Rohatyn – investment banker
- Mark B. Rosenberg – President of Florida International University
- Eugene Rostow – former Dean of Yale Law, legal scholar
- Walt Rostow – National Security Advisor to Lyndon Johnson
- Dean Rusk – 54th Secretary of State of the United States
- Abraham A. Ribicoff – former Democratic Senator from Connecticut
- William V. Roth, Jr. – former Republican Senator of Delaware
- Carl Sagan – American scientist
- Arthur Schlesinger – historian and academic
- Tony Snow – former press-secretary to George W. Bush and journalist
- Ron Silver – actor, director, producer, Co-Founded One Jerusalem
- Strobe Talbott – diplomat
- Cyrus Vance – 57th Secretary of State of the United States
- Vernon A. Walters – United States Army General, former Ambassador of the U.N.
- John Wheeler III – Viet Nam veteran, military consultant, presidential aide; found murdered on December 31st 2010
- Paul Warburg – banker

THE COUNCIL ON FOREIGN RELATIONS

- Caspar Weinberger – 15th Secretary of Defense for the United States
- Albert Wohlstetter
- Roberta Wohlstetter

LIST OF CHAIRMAN:
- Russell Cornell Leffingwell, 1946-53
- John J. McCloy, 1953-70
- David Rockefeller, 1970-85
- Peter G. Peterson, 1985-2007
- Carla A. Hills (Co-Chairman), 2007-present
- Robert E. Rubin (Co-Chairman), 2007-present

LIST OF PRESIDENTS:
- John W. Davis, 1921-33
- George W. Wickersham, 1933-36
- Norman H. Davis, 1936-44
- Russell Cornell Leffingwell, 1944-46
- Allen Welsh Dulles, 1946-50
- Henry Merritt Wriston, 1951-64
- Grayson L. Kirk, 1964-71
- Bayless Manning, 1971-77
- Winston Lord, 1977-85
- John Temple Swing, 1985-93 (Pro tempore)
- Peter Tarnoff, 1986-93
- Alton Frye, 1993
- Leslie Gelb, 1993-2003
- Richard N. Haass, 2003-present

CHAPTER **10**

The Trilateral Commission

IN THE PRECEDING chapter, I gave you a heavy dose of the Council on Foreign Relations, its conspiratorial doctrine, and the effect it has on every aspect of our present and future lives. I hope you will not be bored, but I would be remiss if I did not inform you of the CFR's brother, the Trilateral Commission. As you will see, the Trilateral Commission is concerned with international affairs and policies but has the common objective as the Council on Foreign Relations – a one-world Socialistic, non-religious, and two-class society.

[1] David Rockefeller, Sr. was born on June 12, 1915 and the youngest and only surviving child of John D. Rockefeller. Volumes could and have been written about David Rockefeller but for our purpose, we will say he still heads up the Rockefeller Empire, was a Wall Street Banker, and an international financier (The Illuminati). I will also include the fact that he was the youngest ever to be Director of the Council on Foreign Relations.

In 2002, Rockefeller wrote in his autobiography "Memoirs" that some politicians and economic institutions in America characterized him and his family as internationalists and conspiring with others around the world to build a more integrated global policy and economic structure, a one-world government. "If that's the charge, I stand guilty and am proud of it."

Being dissatisfied with a policy of a "world group," Rockefeller formed the Trilateral Commission in July of 1973. He was deeply influenced by Zbigniew Brzezinski, the National Security Advisor under Jimmy Carter and the author of "Between Two Ages: America's Role in the Technetrotic Era." In his book, Brzezinski praises Marxism, thinks of the United States as obsolete, and praises the formation of a one-world government. As you see, his thinking closely parallels that of "Colonel" Edward Mendell House, founder of the Council on Foreign Relations and Woodrow Wilson's "handler" throughout his Presidency.

As implied earlier, David Rockefeller was very impressed with the philosophy of Brzezinski's book which was replete with statements that Rockefeller believed appropriate. Two examples follow:

[2] On page 72, Brzezinski writes: "Marxism is simultaneously a victory of the external, active man over the inner, passive man and a victory of reason over belief."

On page 83, he states: "Marxism disseminated on the popular level in the form of Communism, represented a major advance in man's ability to conceptualize his relationship to the world."

What Brzezinski fails to tell his readers is that approximately 100 million human beings have been murdered under Marxism "in the form of Communism" just in the twentieth century. It has enslaved a billion more, and has been responsible for those who live in Communist-dominated countries. This shows that Rockefeller wants the same or similar conditions for the world.

[3] Speaking at the Chase Manhattan International Financial Forum in London, Brussels, Montreal, and Paris in early 1972, Rockefeller proposed the creation of an International Commission of Peace and Prosperity (which would later become the Trilateral Commission). Later in 1972 at the Bilderberg meeting, the idea was widely accepted, but elsewhere, it got a cold reception.

Following the above forums and upon the invitation of Rockefeller, Zbigniew Brzezinski, who was already advisor to Rockefeller, left his position of professor at Columbia University to form the Trilateral Commission. Joining him were following high profile Socialists.

- Henry D. Owens (a Foreign Policy Director with the Brookins Institute)
- George S. Franklin
- Robert R. Bowie (of the Foreign Policy Association and Director for International Affairs
- Gerald C. Smith (SALT I negotiator, Rockefeller in-law, and its first North American Chairman
- Marshall Hornblower (former partner at Wilmer Cuter and Picketing
- William Scranton (former Governor of Pennsylvania
- Edwin Reischaller (professor at Harvard University)
- Max Kohnstam (European Policy Center)
- Other founding members included: Alan Greenspan and Paul Volcker, both eventually became Heads of the Federal Reserve System

Rockefeller called his first meeting in July 1972, which was held at his Pocantico Compound in New York's Hudson Valley. Approximately two hundred and fifty individuals attended. All were carefully selected and screened by Rockefeller and represented the very elite of finance and industry. Details of the plans as drawn up by Zbigniew Brzezinski and his group included the formation of world nations into three groups – North America, Europe, and Pacific Asia (originally only Japan). This meeting should not be confused with the first executive meeting which was held in Tokyo in October 1973. The Trilateral Commission was officially initiated and began holding biannual meetings.

[4] The Trilateral Commission Task Force Report, presented at the 1975 meeting in Kyoto, Japan, called An Outline for Remaking World Trade and Finance, said: "Close Trilateral cooperation in keeping the peace, in managing the world economy, and in fostering economic development, and in alleviating world poverty, will improve the chances of a smooth and peaceful evolution of the global system."

Another Commission document said: "The overriding goal is

to make the world safe for independence by protecting the benefits which it provides for each country against external and internal threats which will constantly emerge from those willing to pay a price for more national autonomy. This may sometimes require slowing the pace at which interdependent proceeds, and checking some aspects of it. More frequently, however, it will call for checking the intrusion of national governments into the international exchange of both economic and non-economic goods."

Any intelligent, patriotic American can take many and varied interpretations from the above passage such as the fact that poorer, undeveloped nations must be elevated to a competitive level with, and at the expense of the more advanced nation. A good example is that the overwhelming majority of the United States textile industry was wiped out, contributing to high unemployment and now we cannot compete with the price of goods due to the low wages paid in third-world countries. Another factor we must consider is that manufacturers in the United States pay thirty-five percent taxes while other nations pay fifteen percent or less in taxes. Naturally, our extremely high taxes have been brought about by politicians who, in order to get votes, have allowed lavish retirement benefits and entitlements to union members and Federal employees. We can also see that we are not allowed to manage our own economy despite the fact that we used to be the most innovative and productive country in the world. We also see that with their world power they can produce high and low levels of productivity and subsequent levels of employment. The one that really gets me is that they will assure us that we will pay highly for our autonomy. We have been paying highly since the early part of the Clinton Administration and are now a broke nation with a fourteen-point-four trillion dollar debt. Almost three trillion dollars of the debt has occurred in the past two and one-half years of the Obama Administration and he wants to go even farther into debt by several trillion dollars more. You will note that one of Obama's pet projects is the redistribution of wealth that parallels the Trilateral Commission scheme.

⊰ ONCE THERE WAS AN AMERICA

⁵ We may think we have a choice in electing a President and other key officials but actually we do not. The election of Jimmy Carter is a good example in point. Atlanta, Georgia has long been known as Rockefeller South and David Rockefeller had long-time, close ties to Carter and had, as early as 1971, invited Carter to dine with him at the Chase Manhattan Bank. This was the year that Carter started serving as Governor of Georgia. Incidentally, most of we Georgians call him "The Plains Peanuts Picker" because that is about all he was ever capable of doing.

David Rockefeller and Zbigniew Brzezinski were trying to decide who would become President in 1976. It was necessary that they place a Trilateral-influenced President in the White House and to achieve that, it was necessary to groom an appropriate candidate who would be willing to cooperate with Trilateral aims. Rockefeller was definitely impressed with Carter and it came down to either Carter or Governor Reuben Agnew of Florida being nominated. According to Brzezinski, "It was a close thing between Carter and Agnew, but we were impressed that Carter had opened up trade offices for that State of Georgia in Brussels and Tokyo. That seemed to fit perfectly into the concept of the Trilateral." It did not hurt that Carter was a Founding Member of the Trilateral Commission.

As the campaign for the presidency progressed, it was evident that Carter did not appeal to many Americans. He was far down in practically every public opinion poll. Not to worry, the Trilateral Commission called on its other one-world brothers like the Council on Foreign Relations, the mainstream news media, etc. and Jimmy Carter was elected. Practically everyone, including Leftists, knew that he proved to be the most ineffective President in United States history. If things continue as in the past thirty months, he will lose this title to Barrack Obama.

Before proceeding farter, we need to take a look at what other authorities have to say about the Trilateral Commission:

⁶ Jack Newell and Devy Kidd in "Why a Bankrupt America" state, "The effects of the Council on Foreign Relations and the Trilateral

⊰ 152

THE TRILATERAL COMMISSION ➤

Commission on the affairs of our nation is easy to see. Our own government no longer acts in its own interest, we no longer win any wars we fight, and we constantly tie ourselves to international agreements, pacts, and conventions. And our leaders have developed blatant preferences for Communist Russia, Communist Cuba, and Communist China, while they continue to work for world government which has always been the goal of Communism ... the real goal of our government's leaders is to make the United States into a carbon copy of a Communist State, and merge all nations into a one-world system run by a powerful few."

[7] Senator Barry Goldwater wrote in his book "With No Apologies:" "In my view, the Trilateral Commission represents a skillful, coordinated effort to seize control and consolidate the four centers of power: political, monetary, intellectual, and ecclesiastical. All this to be done in the interest of creating a more peaceful, more productive world community. What the Trilateral Commission truly intends is the creation of a one-world economic power superior to the political governments of the nation-states involved. They believe the abundant materialism they propose to create will overwhelm existing differences. As managers and creators of the system, they will rule the future."

[8] Certain critics such as Alex Jones, an American paleoconservative of "The Obama Deception" documentary claims that the "Commission constitutes a conspiracy seeking to gain control of the United States Government to create a new world order." Mike Thompson, Chairman of the Florida Conservative Union, said: "It puts emphasis on interdependent. Which is a nice euphemism for one-world government."

The number of members of the Trilateral Commission is miniscule when compared to big brother, the Council on Foreign Relations, but its influence is formidable. The membership is divided into numbers proportionate to each of its three regional areas. These members include corporate CEOs, politicians of all major parties, distinguished academics, university presidents, labor union leaders, and not-for-profits involved in overseas philanthropy. Also, members who gain a position in their respective country's government must resign from the Commission. We can be safe to say membership is approximately three hundred and fifty.

The following is a partial list of Americans who are serving as members or have been members of the Trilateral Commission:

CURRENT CHAIRMAN – NORTH AMERICA:
- Joseph S. Nye, Jr. – University Distinguished Professor and former Dean, John F. Kennedy School of Government, Harvard University; former Chair, National Intelligence Council and former U.S. Secretary of Defense for International Security Affairs.

CURRENT DIRECTOR – NORTH AMERICA
- Michael J. O'Neil

FORMER CHAIRMEN – NORTH AMERICA
- Thomas S. Foley (2001-08)
- Paul A. Volcker (1991-2001)
- David Rockefeller (1977-91)
- Gerald C. Smith (1973-77)
- FORMER DIRECTOR – NORTH AMERICA
- Zbigniew Brzezinski

OTHER CURRENT OR PAST MEMBERS – NORTH AMERICA
- John B. Anderson – former United States Congressman
- Bruce Babbitt – Interior Security under Bill Clinton
- Lloyd Bentsen – former United States Senator and Secretary of the Treasury under Bill Clinton
- Tom Bradley – former politician, former Mayor of Los Angeles
- John H. Bryan – former CEO of Sara Lee Bakeries, a Director on Boards of Sara Lee, Goldman Sachs, Bank One, General Motors, and BP.
- James E. Burke – former CEO of Johnson & Johnson

THE TRILATERAL COMMISSION

- George H.W. Bush – former President of the United States
- Warren Christopher – former Secretary of State
- Frank Carlucci – former Secretary of Defense
- Jimmy Carter – former President of the United States
- Dick Cheney – former Vice-President of the United States
- Henry Cisneros – HUD Secretary under Bill Clinton
- Hillary Rodman Clinton – United States Secretary of State
- William Cohen – former Republican Congressman and Senator, U.S. Secretary of Defense under Clinton
- John Danforth – former U.S. Senator
- Hedley Donovan – (deceased) former Editor-in-Chief of Time Magazine, White House Advisor on Domestic and Foreign Policies under Carter, Trilateral Commission founding member
- Lawrence Eagleburg – former Secretary of State under George H.W. Bush
- Daniel J. Evans – former Governor of Washington
- Diane Feinstein – Democratic Senator, former Mayor of San Francisco
- Martin Feldstein – member of the Council on Foreign Relations, Chairman of the Senate Judiciary Subcommittee on Terrorism, Technology, and Homeland Security, Professor of Economics at Harvard University, President and CEO of the National Board of Economic Research, Chairman of the Council of Economic Advisors (1982-84), former Director of the Council on Foreign Relations, member if the Bilderberg Group and the World Economic Forum

The list goes on in like manner throughout the alphabet and by now you should not be surprised to see names of the most notable figures in America, such as Henry Kissinger, Alan Greenspan, etc.

These members are indeed respectable to the unknowing and prominent Americans by practically all standards. I ask the question – are they? Does deliberately destroying one's own government and the way of life of its people propel them to such lofty positions?

CHAPTER **11**

The United Nations and the Mainstream Media

THE UNITED NATIONS:

[1] The League of Nations failed to prevent World War II (1939-1945) and because of widespread recognition the humankind could not afford a Third World War, the United Nations was established to replace the severely flawed League of Nations.

The earliest concrete plans for a new world organization began under the sponsorship of the U.S. State Department in 1939. Franklin D. Roosevelt, Council on Foreign Relations member, first coined the term "United Nations" as a term to describe the Allied Countries. The term was first officially used on January 1, 1942 when twenty-six governments signed the Atlantic Charter, pledging to continue the war effort.

On April 25, 1945, the United Nations Conference on International Organization began in San Francisco, attended by fifty governments and a number of non-government organizations involved in drafting the Charter of the United Nations. Six months later the United Nations came into existence on October 24, 1945.

By definition, we can say the United Nations is an international organization that no one person can explain it. Therefore, I will shorten it by saying there are currently one hundred and ninety-two member states in the world, the United Nations, and its specialized

THE UNITED NATIONS AND THE MAINSTREAM MEDIA

agencies decide on substantive and administrative issues in regular meetings held throughout the year.

The following paragraphs sound worthy, humane, and intended for those who are gullible have been so unconcerned they failed to search beyond the façade of this illegitimate organization. The true purpose of the United Nations is to serve as vehicle to carry out the plans of the Evil Octopus (The Illuminati/International Bankers) for world control.

There has been valid opposition to the United Nations, even before its existence in 1945. Although I cannot remember the name of the report or find evidence of it, I recall a report issued about 1946-47 wherein it was found that only two members of Congress voted against the United States becoming a member of the U.N.. The report also stated that these two individuals were the only members of Congress who actually read the United Nations Charter.

[2] Since the late 1900's there has been a growing movement in the United States to withdraw from the United Nations. Several notable proponents like U.S. Representatives John Duncan of Tennessee, Terry Everett of Alabama, and Samuel Johnson of Texas, all of who co-sponsored or supported HR1146 claim that the United Nations subverts American sovereignty. Unfortunately, HR1146 did not receive much support from other legislators who were either ignorant, uncaring, or part of problem.

Utah state legislator, Don Bush, claims that many programs of the United Nations have violated the U.S. Constitution, such as the implementation of the International Court of Justice and the Laws of the Sea Treaty, both of which the United States does not "currently" endorse.

To show how little our politicians care about public opinion a Rasmussen Report in 2004 showed that only forty-four percent of the United States Citizens had a favorable view of the United Nations. This number continued to decline steadily, and in 2006 the number had fallen to thirty-one percent and the probability of the United Nations continues to decline to this day.

◄ ONCE THERE WAS AN AMERICA

A controversial incident occurred in 1992 when U.S. Army medic, Michael New protested the United Nations by refusing to wear the U.N. insignia on his uniform during a peacekeeping mission to Macedonia. Michael New faced a court martial and was subsequently discharged for disobedience to his commanding officer; to this day, New still has the belief that he was correct to refuse serving under the United Nations forces during the Korean War. Among my twenty-four awards and decorations is the United Nations Medal, which I was ashamed to wear after uncovering the real truth of the United Nations.

When withdrawal from the United Nations is mentioned, response from most people is that they think such action is isolationism. Naturally, they are totally wrong. Unilateralism has long been part of our history and we do not have to belong to a world organization to maintain it. George Washington warned that the United States should "steer clear of permanent alliances with any portion of the foreign world." We have gained nothing by being a member of the United Nations. Instead, it has been a constant financial drain on our country, taken us into necessary wars which cost thousands upon thousands of American lives.

[3] To show the financial drain on the United States by participation in the United Nations, we have to understand that there are two U.N. Budgets. First, there is the Regular Budget that finances the General Assembly, the Security Council, the Economic and Social Council, the International Court of Justice, and the Secretariat. It also finances that U.N.'s special political missions; the largest are the United Nations Mission in Afghanistan and Iraq. The second budget is the Peacekeeping Budget who assessment formula is the same as the Regular Budget, but gives greater discounts to poorer nations. The deficit is compensated by the five permanent members of the Security Council consisting of the United States, United Kingdom, France, Russia, and China. The math on the Regular Budget is very fussy but it amounts to a few billion dollars per year. The Peacekeeping Budget is clearer and we will concentrate on it.

THE UNITED NATIONS AND THE MAINSTREAM MEDIA

[4] The General Assembly apportions peacekeeping expenses based on a special scale of assessment under a complex formula that Member States themselves have established. This formula takes into account, among other things, the relative economic wealth of Member States, with the five permanent members of the Security Council required to pay a larger share.

The budget for United Nations Peacekeeping operations for the fiscal year of July 1, 2010 to June 30, 2011 is about seven-point-eighty-three billion dollars.

The top ten providers of assisted contributions to Peacekeeping Operations in 2011-12 are as follows:

1. United States – 27.14% (has been negotiated down to a bit over 22%)
2. Japan – 12.53%
3. United Kingdom – 8.15%
4. Germany – 8.02%
5. France – 7.55%
6. Italy – 5.00%
7. China – 3.93%
8. Canada – 3.21%
9. Spain – unclear (about 3%)
10. Republic of Korea – 2.26%

As you see, the United States is currently paying about one-fourth of the entire budget. For most years (before the recent reduction), the U.S. paid more than one-fourth of the budget. You will also note that of the remaining one hundred and sixty-one nations, some pay very little and a few pay practically nothing.

This is a considerable amount of money for a nation that is broke and trying to raise our debt ceiling in order to stay afloat. It is your money being spent on a worthless cause. If you do not agree with me now, I believe many will change their minds before we leave this subject. Oh! I forgot, did you notice that China who holds the biggest part of our national debt of fourteen-point-four billion dollars pays only three-point-ninety-three percent while we have usually paid twenty-seven-point-fourteen percent?

Even though we pay one-fourth of the combined budgets of the United Nations, we have limited power, with the exception of being on the Security Council as a permanent member. This council consists of fifteen member states with five as permanent members consisting of the United States, China, France, Germany, and the United Kingdom. These permanent members each have veto power over substantive but not over procedural resolutions allowing a permanent member to block but not to block the debate of a resolution unacceptable to it.

Anyone who watches newscasts on television, listens to the radio, or reads a newspaper knows that when the United States tries to resolve a serious problem, they are vetoed either by China or Russia (sometimes France). The Iraqi War is one example. Time-after-time, Saddam Hussein ignored sanctions over weapons of mass destruction. When the United States pushed for harsher enforcement, we were constantly blocked. The same is true with the current situation in Iran. We know that they are just a few steps away from becoming a nuclear power, vowing to destroy Israel. The only thing the United States can get out of the United Nations is meaningless sanctions that Iran promptly ignores.

As we have learned, the United States has one vote. So does Chad, Angola, or any of the one hundred and sixty-one other members. Even though we have given aid to all of these nation states, most of them show disdain or outright hatred toward the U.S. by constantly voting against almost any action we propose.

The foregoing paragraphs pose the question as to why we are members of an organization that we unfairly support financially and from which we receive no benefits. The answer is simple: we are to be brought down to a lower level of power by exhausting our resources. Remember: it is your taxes being spent by compliant or ignorant politicians. These billions of dollars we spend each year could be

THE UNITED NATIONS AND THE MAINSTREAM MEDIA ▶

used for other, more worthy causes. One more statistic on the subject: From 1948 to June 2010, the cost of United Nations Peacekeeping alone amounts to sixty-four billion dollars. Our twenty-seven-point-fourteen percent (now twenty-two percent) of this amount would look very good if applied to our unsustainable national debt. Again, you must remember that this does not include the billions that went into the United Nations Regular Account.

When not with an overwhelming majority of American troops and under the command of American officers, it is hard to find meaningful successes of the United Nations. [5] The U.N. has been successful in humanitarian relief efforts (handing out supplies and food) in Somalia and the former Socialist Yugoslavia. It has also been successful in negotiating disputes in some African nations.

Failures of the United Nations Peacekeeping are so plentiful that we can easily say that the U.N., as a whole, is a dismal failure. The failures are too numerous and too detailed to list; however, the following will give you a good snapshot of the failures:

[6] During the 1994 Rwanda Genocide, United Nations Peacekeepers stood by as the Hutus slaughtered more than eight million Tutsis within a one hundred day period. Afterwards, the blue helmeted U.N. troops displayed their previously known lawlessness. One incident involved Belgian U.N. troops who tricked a large group of Tutsis by arranging a meal in the dining hall of a large refugee camp then slipping away to notify the Hutus who then slaughtered the entire group of Tutsis.

[7] In December 2004, during the United Nations Peacekeeping mission in Congo, at least sixty-eight cases of rape, prostitution, and pedophilia were reported. More than one hundred other allegations have been uncovered by United Nations investigators. Many of the crimes were horrible, like gouging out the eyes of young boys who tried to keep their even younger sisters from being raped, gang rape of women and children, chopping off heads, etc. According to United Nations' investigators, all such crimes were perpetrated by U.N. Peacekeepers, specifically ones from Poland, Uruguay, Morocco,

Tunisia, South Africa, and Napal. Also in the same month, a French logistician expert was charged of the rape of a child and child pornography. In a Reuters release dated October 1, 2010, it was revealed that the United Nations had issued a report documenting atrocities in the Democratic Republic of Congo between 1993 and 2003. The five hundred and sixty page report found that all combatant forces systematically used rape and sexual assault on women and children. Sexual violence was a daily reality for Congolese women. It was brutal and sometimes driven by ethnic hatred. Children were particularly vulnerable to such violence, including rape and murder. These crimes were committed by United Nations forces from Rwanda, Burundi, Uganda, Angola, Zimbabwe, Nambia, Chad, and Sudan. It also lists cases where Zairian or Congolese security forces were responsible for the violation of human rights.

[8] During the Bosnian War in 1993, the United Nations declared the town of Srebrenica a "safe haven" under U.N. protection and positioned four hundred (some say six hundred) [9] U.N. Dutch blue helmets to protect the town. In 1995, the town was attacked and captured by the Army of Republike Srpaka. The U.N. Dutch were ineffective, the United Nations failed to send in more soldiers. Consequently, the Srebrenica Massacre began, resulting in the killing of eight thousand Bosnian Muslims. A paramilitary unit from Serbia known as Scorpio and the Greek Volunteers also participated in the massacre.

The majority of those killed were adult men and teenage boys, but the victims included boys under age fifteen, men over sixty-five, women, young girls, and infants. All male Muslim prisoners were stripped of their personal belongings (including clothing) or means of identification and were methodically killed. The Bosnian Federal Commission of Missing Persons contains eight thousand three hundred and seventy-three names, approximately five hundred of them under the age of fifteen and including several dozen women and children. As of June 2011, six thousand five hundred and ninety-four genocide victims have been identified by DNA analysis of body parts

THE UNITED NATIONS AND THE MAINSTREAM MEDIA

recovered from mass graves.

I could continue with many, many more cases of crimes committed by the United Nations Peacekeepers who have become known as "Beasts in Blue Berets." These crimes have occurred in almost every U.N. operation. They consist of any imaginable crime, such as raping infants, gang raping pre-teen girls and women of all ages, beheading, eye-gouging, throat-slitting, forcing children to drink vomit and poison, cutting off male genitals, etc. It is well-known that wherever U.N. Peacekeepers set up operations, prostitution rings are set up by members of a United Nations unit and if there are no willing prostitutes, young girls will be rounded up for this purpose. These crimes are not only committed by third-world countries since we can include Canada, Belgium, France, and others.

All of these atrocities are fairly well-known to the whole world but have been downplayed by high officials of the United Nations (and the U.S. controlled news media), who have given a watered down report many years after the event. Regardless of the downplaying, it does not relieve responsible citizens and nations of taking action by demanding that their respective countries get out of the United Nations. Until we do, we are as guilty as the German citizens who allowed Hitler to kill millions of Jewish citizens

I ask you: how would you feel if United Nations Peacekeepers were deployed to patrol the streets of towns and cities of the United States? Do you say it will never happen? We are dangerously close to a one-world government. When it happens and there is an uprising, you well could find U.N. Peacekeepers from Uganda, Congo, Belgium, etc. occupying your town or city. The irony of this is that you have paid for this with your taxes and continue to do so. Most of you sit on your duff and refuse to get involved in taking back your lost country. Remember that the United States has set the precedent for it by going into other countries under the banner of the United Nations, while the politicians you elected say nothing and are so stupid or uninformed that they do not have a clue as to what is happening.

THE MAINSTREAM MEDIA:

In our discussion of the mainstream media, we will primarily be looking at the bias, the political leaning, and the ownership and control of the media.

Unless you have been living under a rock or have no concept of the precarious situation that our nation is in, you surely must know that the mainstream media leans drastically far to the left, which is in opposition to our Constitutional Republic. This is not a new trend since it has been going on for many decades and is another tentacle of The Evil Octopus (The Illuminati/International Bankers).

[10] In 1981, S. Robert Lichter of George Washington University and Stanley Rothman of Smith College – both extremely liberal institutions – released a then groundbreaking survey of two hundred and forty journalists at the most influential national media outlets, including the New York Times, Washington Post, Time, Newsweek, U.S. News and World Report, ABC, CBS, NBC, and PBS on the political attitudes and voting patterns. The media elite votes of 1964-1976 were as follows:

- 1964 – 94% Democrat
- 1968 – 86% Democrat
- 1972 – 81% Democrat
- 1976 – 81% Democrat

[11] Recent percentage remains about the same but there appears to be a fast growing trend to the left – this was especially true during the 2008 Presidential Election. Survey after survey shows more than eighty percent of the media describes themselves as liberal. As we proceed, keep in mind that [12] "the term media bias implies a pervasive or widespread bias contravening the standards of journalism." In my opinion, this eighty-to-eight-five percent number of so-called journalists in television and the print media are not journalists at all – they are political assassins. They possess sick, evil, warped minds and pose as journalists, and it does not matter how you look at it, they are

THE UNITED NATIONS AND THE MAINSTREAM MEDIA ➤

a disgrace to their profession.

[13] A number of journalists have openly admitted that the majority of their brethren approach the news from a liberal angle. During the 2004 Presidential Campaign for example, Newsweek's Evan Thomas predicted that sympathetic media coverage would boost Kerry's vote by "maybe fifteen percent"

Surveys of journalists' self-reported voting habits show them backing the Democratic candidates in every Presidential Election since 1964. A poll conducted by the University of Connecticut found journalists backed John Kerry over George W. Bush by greater than a two-to-one margin. There have been some estimates that journalists backed Barrack Obama almost unanimously over John McCain. Although these so-called journalists love to spew their biases, they also do it to please their superiors and owners who are of the same ilk.

[14] A study by UCLA was conducted to find which media outlets were either to the right of center or left of center. Of the twenty major outlets studied, eighteen scored left of center, with CBS's Evening News, the New York Times and the Los Angeles Times ranking second, third, and fourth most liberal behind the news pages of the Wall Street Journal.

The United States Government's deregulation of the telecommunications industry has resulted in a rushing wave of corporate acquisition and mergers that have already produced several huge media conglomerates, with others continuing to appear. As a result, practically every television program you watch, every movie you see, every radio program you hear, every newspaper, magazine, or book you read, and the music you buy are all produced by these conglomerates. All are liberal to say the least, but we can go farther by saying they control the minds of the average citizen. They want to downgrade morality and want to destroy the Christian religion. Naturally, the owners have a common bond with Wall Street Bankers so you know what that means.

Unless there are some unknown changes, [15] seven men run the vast majority of United States television networks, the printed media, the Hollywood movie industry, the book publishing industry, and the music recording industry. Most of these individuals are bundled into huge media conglomerates run by the following seven individuals:

1. Gerald Levin, CEO and Director of AOL Time Warner
2. Michael Eisner, Chairman and CEO of Walt Disney Company
3. Edgar Bronfman, Sr., Chairman of Seagram Company Ltd
4. Edgar Bronfman, Jr., President and CEO of Seagram Company Ltd and Head of Universal Studios
5. Sumner Redstone, Chairman and CEO of Viacom, Inc.
6. Dennis Dammerman, Vice-Chairman of General Electric
7. Peter Chenin, President and Co-CEO of News Corporation Limited

[16] "These seven men collectively control ABC, NBC, CBS, the Turner Broadcasting System, CNN, MTV, Universal Studios, MCA Records, Geffen Records, DGC Records, GRP Records, Rising Times Records, Curb-Universal Records, and Interscope Records. Most of the larger independent newspapers are owned by similar interests as well."

We could continue with much more evidence of Anti-American liberal media control and the brainwashing of most Americans but I believe you have been given enough so that you will see the truth. We may think we are free, but are we? We may think we have a choice when voting for a President or other high-ranking politicians, but do we? I think not, for most people. Hopefully, this book will sell well and many will become educated in what actually is happening – this is my only purpose for writing it. Now is the time to rock-and-roll, so wake up, shake up, and break up the system and get our country back.

CHAPTER **12**

The Obama Tragedy

BEFORE PROCEEDING WITH this and the following chapter, I should provide you with more about myself than you will see on the front and back covers of this book. This is not for egotistical reasons; instead, it is for clarity in the way that I describe conditions, individuals, and events.

I am a patriotic American. In our present society, this makes a far right winger to the controlled media and the improperly informed portion of the populace. I am a realist. In my earlier years, and due to ignorance, I was a Democrat. After becoming educated (not from colleges or universities), I became a Conservative. I am not a Republican. However, during most of my adult life, I have voted Republican and contributed money to their party since they are the lesser of two evils. I cry when I see the American flag flying and hear the National Anthem. I do the same when I hear the singing of God Bless America. I devoted twenty-seven years of my life in military service and it makes me sad, and sometimes furious, when I see (primarily ignorant) Hollywood and television celebrities, comedians, and politicians openly degrade our country. I am a Christian, which mean I believe in God The Father, God The Son, and God The Holy Spirit. Because of this belief, I am not a racist nor am I Anti-Jewish.

I am able to manage my time in such a manner that I can devote time to God, time to doing the most I can to regain our country, and time for personal pleasure. I am a spectator sports nut and my wife and I go out for dinner and dancing about twice a week. We also travel extensively, both in the United States and many other parts of the world. I was never a stick in the mud person and did many of the wrong things in my early, wild years.

You may recall the third paragraph in Chapter One wherein I stated that the climax of the fall of the United States occurred in November of 2008. Naturally, I was referring to the election of Barrack Obama as President of the United States of America. It is still amazing to me how citizens of the supposedly most enlightened country in the world could blindly follow such a person with a politically shallow and radical background. There was a plethora of information on him that was easily accessible, but as I have said before, American citizens have evolved into such a state of apathy that they will not take the time or make the effort to be concerned with the welfare of our once great nation.

One can understand the Far Left, Radical Democrats following such a flawed individual since they hate America and want to see our Republic with its free enterprise system replaced by a Socialist form of government where the government takes care of every whim. They care nothing about individual integrity, drive, and pride in achievement. What is hard to understand is those individuals who otherwise would not have followed Obama like the rats followed the Pied Piper into the Wesser River in Hamelin, Germany in 1284 (this is folklore based on a true story).

Approximately seventy-three percent of our population did not believe in abortion as espoused by Obama. Regardless of this fact, a huge percentage of these people threw away their moral and religious beliefs and voted for this evil man who, in actuality, hates or at least detests America. There is an explanation for this which we will later discuss.

I may not be the sharpest tack in the box, but when I observed Obama as the keynote speaker during the Democratic National Convention held in Boston during July 2004, I sensed something

THE OBAMA TRAGEDY

ominous about him. Shortly thereafter, I began researching his background and, needless to say, I did not like what I found. Since becoming President, I have seen more and more of his duplicity and inadequacies. This also makes me wonder why Conservative Republicans did not pick up on the sinister personality of this person.

Psychologists unanimously agree that childhood experience affect personality in one's adult life. Psychologists also agree that a person is affected by their experiences, education, and associations during the formative years. These formative years may extend as far as their early twenties. Accordingly, it will be enlightening to go into many aspects of Barrack Obama's early childhood and other formative years.

[1] Obama's father, Barrack Hussein Obama, Sr., abandoned his wife and family in Kenya, travelled to Hawaii and enrolled in the University of Hawaii in September of 1959. Obama's mother, Stanley Ann Durham, also a student at the University of Hawaii met Obama, Sr. on campus, became pregnant, and married him on February 2, 1961. The marriage was performed without Obama, Sr. divorcing his Kenyan wife, thus the marriage was bigamous. Despite what the birthers say, Barrack Hussein Obama, Jr. was born on August 4, 1961, six months after the marriage of his parents. To me there is no doubt – he is an American citizen.

Shortly after Obama's birth, his mother took him to Seattle, Washington where she took courses at the University of Washington from September 1961 to June 1962. Due to his shallow character, Obama, Sr. again abandoned a wife and son, going to Cambridge, Massachusetts to begin classes at Harvard University in September 1962.

Obama's mother returned to Hawaii in January 1963 where Obama was raised by his white grandparents until 1967. His mother divorced Obama, Sr. in 1964 and, in June 1965, she married a Muslim named Lolo Soetoro who was an Indonesian surveyor. Lolo returned to Indonesia in 1966. During the one year period of 1965-66, Obama switched back and forth between his black stepfather and his white grandparents.

As we see, Obama bounced around like a rubber ball because of a worthless, Socialist black father and a far left Socialist, hippie, Atheist mother. Pitch in white grandparents and a black stepfather and there must have been chaos in the mind of the five year old boy. Needless to say, these early childhood experiences were confusing, traumatic, and definitely had a damaging effect on his character and personality in his adult years.

During the month of October 1967, Obama and his mother moved to Jakarta to rejoin Lolo Soetoro. This was a move that had a drastic effect on Barrack Obama, Jr. for the next four years. It shaped much of the beliefs, radical thinking, and personality disorders that we see in him as an adult.

Lolo Soetoro was a devout Muslim who introduced Obama to Islam very gradually while in Hawaii. Upon arrival in Jakarta, Lolo continued to educate Obama in the Islam faith on a gradual plan. During the four years in Jakarta, Obama attended St. Francis Assai School from 1968-70 and State Elementary School from 1970-71, becoming well-indoctrinated in Islamic teachings and culture. In both schools, he was registered as Barry Soetoro and his religion was listed as Islam. In addition to the instruction from grades first through fourth, Obama attended mosque prayer services with Lolo almost daily. In the evenings, Obama sat with local government workers, activists, and politicians, getting plenty of guidance in Socialism, anti-colonialism, and white hatred.

In mid-1971, with his impressionable ten year old mind packed with Muslim ideology, Socialism, a strong taste of anti-colonialism and conflict with his race mixture, Obama moved back to Hawaii to live with his white grandparents. He was enrolled in the prestigious Punahou (private) School in the fifth grade and continued his education there until receiving his high school diploma in 1979.

In December 1971, Barrack Obama, Sr. visited Hawaii, which for all practical purposes was the first time Obama, Jr. had seen his father. It also proved to be the last time Obama would see his father.

However, the event made a deep impression on Obama that lasts to the present time.

As you probably know, Obama, Sr. was a failure in most parts of his life. He was a bigamist, an alcoholic, and a loud-mouthed, argumentative, radical filled with white hate toward the United States, Europe, and all white people in general. He failed to achieve anything more than a low to mid level government job because of his drunkenness and sexual promiscuity. He was also forced to leave Harvard University before completing his doctorate, again because of his drinking and excessive sexual activity, yet he insisted that he be addressed as Doctor. Despite these character faults, he was a slick, conniving, charming actor and speaker when sober. These appear to be traits Obama, Jr. inherited from his father.

During his visit to Hawaii in December of 1971, Obama, Sr. was invited to speak at Punahoe School. Displaying his arrogant, showy personality, he came dressed as an African Tribal Chief and, with his captivating speech, had the students in the palm of his hand with enchanting stories of his exploits in Africa. Needless to say, Obama, Jr. was bursting with pride and for weeks thereafter, he was told by others students how lucky he was to have such a father. Also during his visit, Obama, Sr. planted more seeds of anti-colonialism and hatred for all white people in the mind of his son.

During high school, we see more the emerging Obama displaying some of the characteristics of his father. He was a bit more mature than his classmates with this coming from his earlier indoctrination by his stepfather and other adults in Jakarta. He gained his identity, "declaring himself black." His fellow students later told the Honolulu Star-Banner that he often attended parties and other events in order to associate with African American college students and U.S. military service personnel.

[2] In his book, "Dreams From My Father," Obama admits to drinking alcohol, smoking pot and cocaine, but denies taking heroin while in high school, but not afterwards. I seriously doubt that this is true when I look at his actions and associates while attending

liberal institutions like Occidental College, Columbia University, and Harvard University, all known for their students being "potheads" and "crack heads."

[3] In "Dreams From My Father," Obama also wrote of a friend who he only identifies as "Frank." Even though Obama thought he was skillfully hiding "Frank's" identity, he left clues that were easily followed by a prominent and trusted journalist. The mysterious "Frank" in Obama's secret political life turns out to be his high school mentor, Frank Marshall Davis. This association came about easily since Davis had a frienship with Obama's grandparents. Frank Marshall Davis was a newspaper journalist, poet, labor activist, and a well-known Communist.

Frank Marshall Davis had moved to Hawaii in 1948 and was in his late sixties when he became Obama's mentor. The relationship was that of a father and son, and apparently Obama eagerly swallowed Davis' philosophy down to the smallest particle and continues to hold onto and use them when the opportunity arises. Davis helped Obama plan his future political career and enabled his dislike or hatred for white people; however, Davis also taught Obama how to manipulate and use them.

By now, most Americans know the way Obama manipulates the truth, tells half-truths, says something on one day and denies it the next. Therefore, when he admit to his association with "Frank," attending Socialist conferences, and involvement with Marxist literature, but denies being a hardcore academic Marxist, we can rest assured that he was deeper involved than he admits.

After graduating from high school in Hawaii in 1979, Obama finished his freshman and sophomore years (1979-81) at the very liberal Occidental College in Los Angeles. [4] An interesting report came from a Graduate Teaching Assistant at Occidental College in late 1980 who said, "My most vivid memories of my time visiting with Obama was that he strongly argued a rather simple-minded version of Marxist theory. I remember he was passionate about his point-of-view. As I remember, he was articulating the same Marxist theory taught by various professors at Occidental College."

While at Occidental College, Obama followed the pattern he used at Punahoe High School by seeking out the most radical professors and students. 5 A good example is his chosen house-mate: a wealthy Pakistani Muslim named Mohammed Hasan Chandoo. We will see this same pattern throughout his studies at Columbia and Harvard. As easily seen, he continues to follow this pattern to the present time.

Even though the following information no longer concerns Obama's formative years, we will start when he was a student at Columbia University.

Throughout the 2008 Presidential Campaign, the subject frequently came up concerning Obama's association with the American-hating terrorist, Bill Ayers. Obama always brushed it away by saying his relationship with Ayers was extremely casual and their contacts were few. 6 An article by Jack Kelly in the Pittsburgh Post-Gazette suggests that Obama and Bill Ayers have a much closer relationship that is well known and goes back to Obama's college days at Columbia University where Bill Ayers was a graduate student. I can believe they had a relationship since it follows Obama's pattern of seeking out the most radical students and faculty on campuses. An additional reason for this belief is that Obama admits his first campaign for the Illinois Senate began in Bill Ayers' living room. Additional information follows:

In 1995, Bill Ayers was instrumental in the selection of Obama, then a junior attorney at a second-tier law firm. Chairman of the Chicago Annenberg Challenge, and education "reform" project that spent one hundred and ten million dollars to no apparent effect, other than providing employment to otherwise unemployed radicals.

A few years later, Michelle Obama and Bernadette Dorn, also a convicted terrorist and Bill Ayers' wife, worked at the same time for the Chicago law firm Gidney Austin. As discussed earlier, there was a probable prior relationship between Obama and Ayers, so it stands to reason there was likely a relationship between the couples during this period of time. We will see more related information a bit later.

Investigative reporter Jack Cahill has noted some intriguing coincidences between Obama's 1995 autobiography, "Dreams From My Father," and Ayers' 2007 book, "Fugitive Days," for which Obama wrote a dust jacket blurb. Both books have the same lyrical style and are filled with nautical imagery which would come naturally from Ayers, who spent a year as a merchant seaman, but appears nowhere else in Obama's writing.

Both Obama and Ayers spoke at a testimonial dinner for Rashid Khalidi, a former member of the Palestine Liberation Network. Obama and Khalidi lived close to each other in the faculty zone at the University of Chicago and dined together a number of times and it was reported that the Obama's babysat for the Khalidi children.

In the 1996 campaign for the Illinois Senate, Obama sought and received the endorsement of the New Party, a creation of the Democratic Socialist of America. This party was so to the left that the Green Party described it as fringe.

We can conclude that a huge number of Obama's radical associates, which would include Moveon.org, George Soros and practically all of his cabinet, appointed czars, political and judicial appointments, are the same American-hating Socialist or Socialist-leaning types that he has sought out during his entire life.

[7] For twenty years, Obama sat in Jeremiah Wright's Church, Trinity United Church of Christ, where Wright spewed his venom toward white Americans and hatred for the United States of America in his weekly sermons. Wright teaches his black congregation that they should not sing "God Bless America." Instead, he instructs them to sing "God Damn America." When faced with this fact, Obama had the audacity to lie like a sneak thief by saying he was not in attendance when Wright used such language. This is ridiculous, since Wright preached vicious white hatred and disdain for America in practically every sermon.

An ABC News review of dozens of Wright's sermons offered for sale by the church, found repeated denunciations of the United States based on what he, Wright, described as his reading of the Gospel and the treatment of black Americans

"The government gives them the drugs, builds bigger prisons, passes a three-strike law and then wants us to sing 'God Bless America.' No, No, No, God Damn America, that's in the Bible for killing innocent people," Wright said in a 2003 sermon. "God Damn America for treating our citizens as less than human. God Damn America for as long as she acts like she is God and she is supreme."

In addition to damning America, Wright told his congregation on the Sunday after September 11, 2001 that the United States brought on Al Quada's attack because of its own terrorism.

It is apparent that Obama shares the views of Wright. If he did not, he would not have sat through such evil, Anti-American, Anti-Christian garbage. Obama left Wright's church only after it began to hurt his campaign for the Presidency. Before leaving Wright's church, Obama said, "I don't think my church is actually particularly controversial." Fine words from the President of the United States, don't you think?

Obama has stated that Wright was a father figure and helped him in many ways. Don't forget while Wright was passionately spewing such filth from his vulgar mouth, Barrack and Michelle Obama were married by this evil being. The Obama's also thought it proper that Wright baptize their two daughters and is credited by Obama for the title of his book, "The Audacity of Hope."

[8] We must not overlook Obama's first visit to Kenya where he stood at his father's grave and made a pact with himself to carry on what Obama, Sr. wanted to accomplish. Accordingly, most reasonable thinking people see that Obama, Sr.'s dream became Obama, Jr.'s dreams, the latter wants to bring the United States down to a third-world country. We also know Obama, Sr. was a loud mouth, unaccomplished person who was always injecting himself into tribal politics, causing discord and, in general, being a nuisance who was detested by most tribesmen. He was a multiple bigamist, an arrogant, argumentative drunk who had several car wrecks before he finally,

in essence, killed himself in a drunken vehicle crash. This is the man whose dreams our President has taken for his own dreams. Look around and think a bit. How much of Obama's dream has come true in the past two and one-half years.

[9] Barrack Obama admits showing interest in Black Muslim faith by reading Farrakhan's letter and his activities from his, Obama's, twenties. Obama's interest in Farrakhan certainly is more than a passing fancy. In addition, Obama associated with many followers of Farrakhan, to include his twenty-year relationship with Jeremiah Wright, one of Farrakhan's strongest supporters. Obama thought so favorably of him that he joined Farrakhan's 1995 March on Washington, D.C. Reportedly, Obama joined Al Sharpton and Jeremiah Wright in organizing the march.

Lastly, Obama was an ardent follower of the teachings of Saul Alinsky, a neo-Marxist and the father of modern day radicals, who is known for showing how the have-nots can take it all from those that have. His book, "Rules for Radicals," is a fine work on community deception in organization. Obama swallowed every word and has followed Alinsky's teachings without fail.

[10] Obama spent years teaching workshops on the Alinsky method. In 1985, he began a four-year period as a community organizer in Chicago, working for an Alinskyite group called the Development Communities Project.

Obama served as a paid director of the Woods Foundation from 1999 to December 2002 and provided startup funding and later capital to the Midwest Alinsky Academy. Near the anniversary of Alinsky's one hundredth birthday, Alinsky's son wrote a letter to the gathering of radicals and stated, in part, "Obama learned his lesson well, I am proud to see that my father's model for organizing is being applied successfully beyond local community organizing to affect the Democratic Campaign in 2008."

In recent months, Obama is openly being called a Socialist, by prominent, respected individuals in industry, politics, and even in some news media – other than Fox News. Then of course the question,

"Is Obama really a Socialist?" comes about more often. The answer is a resounding YES. However, he is much more than the run-of-the-mill Socialist and, in many ways, a very dangerous man for the position he holds. You must remember most human beings carry their childhood and formative year beliefs throughout most of their lives. Obama is a standard Socialist with a bit of Fabian Socialism thrown in. He is without doubt a racist, Anti-Colonist, Anti-Israel, pro-Muslim, narcissist who is unethical and untrustworthy.

His Pro-Muslim stance goes as far back as his school days and burst out on his trip to the Mid-East where he groveled at the feet of Arab leaders which was a shocking disgraceful embarrassment to the Office of the Presidency. This came natural to him because of his background and true self. He had no right to apologize to these people for perceived shortcomings by America, after all, the only thing we have done is prop up their economies while they bleed us dry by oil price-gouging.

I initially accepted Obama as a Socialist along the lines of a Franklin D. Roosevelt, but the more I studied, the more complex his identity became. I had all the ingredients but I kept overlooking his anti-colonialism until I read Dinesh D'Souza's book, "The Roots of Obama's Rage." I strongly recommend this book to every American citizen and it should be required reading for every member of Congress.

As a Socialist, Obama wants a huge federal government that has control of all aspects of our lives. He wants the populace disenfranchised and dependent upon the federal government for every need. Naturally, this does away with our free enterprise, Capitalistic society that has been the best system known to mankind. You must remember the graveyard pact wherein his dreams are the dreams he got from the study of his father. We know his father was a hate-filled, Anti-Colonist who considered the United States and European countries, especially England, as the cause of all of Africa's problems and shortcomings. Barrack Obama is just as full of hate and wants America broken down to a third-world country. In this endeavor, he is making great strides.

◄ ONCE THERE WAS AN AMERICA

In two and one-half years, he has spent more than every president from George Washington through Ronald Reagan with a fourteen-point-four trillion dollar national debt.

As I write this chapter, Obama wants the National Debt Ceiling raised by three or more trillion dollars without cutting his reckless spending. He is devoid of leadership and keeps the situation in turmoil. If a solution to our current credit ceiling is not resolved within the next four days, our credit rating will be lowered to that of a third-world country, which we have seen evidence and reasons that this is his goal. (Since initially writing this, our credit rating has been lowered for the first time in our history and we are now on the level of the small island of Bermuda).

The recently Republican-controlled House of Representatives is the only government entity making any effort in resolving this problem. They have passed two bills that would have provided a higher debt ceiling with corresponding cuts in spending. Both bills were tabled immediately by the Democratic-controlled Senate without a word of discussion. The Speaker of the House and Democratic senators prepared a bi-partisan bill that Obama said he would sign. However, upon presentation, he refused to sign it. Additionally and as of this date, it has been eight hundred and twenty days or two-point-twenty-five years that Obama and the Democrats have gone without presenting an annual budget. This is the responsibility of the President and Obama has no plan or apparently no knowledge of how to prepare the annual budget. He has no solution for lowering our unsustainable national debt and continues to even look at the House Republican plans which are well-prepared and without doubt are very workable.

In order to show more of Obama's anti-colonialism and white hatred we should take a look at the shoddy treatment he openly and purposely imposed upon the British Prime Minister during this visit to the White House.

[11] The Daily Telegraph stated, "President Obama has been rudeness personified toward Britain. His handling of the Prime Minister,

Gordon Brown, was appalling."

The list of offenses is quite long. First, Obama cancelled a podium-to-podium news conference with Brown and also recently removed a bust of former Prime Minister Winston Churchill from the Oval Office. This was a stinging blow to one of history's greatest leaders, to England and the United States, since through many decades, wars and international conflicts, England has been our strongest ally. Obama simply could not show any tact and diplomacy because of his racist nature and Anti-Colonist hatred, even though colonialism is long past.

Adding further insult to the Prime Minister's visit was the cheap and thoughtless gift our "magnificent" President gave to Prime Minister Brown.

Prime Minster Brown clearly took care in choosing his gift for Obama, presenting him with a pen holder crafted from the timbers of the Nineteenth century British warship HMS President. The HMS President's sister ship HMS Resolute had previously provided the wood for the Oval Office's desk. The Prime Minister's gift was clearly not a last minute thought.

Showing absolutely no class and outright disdain for our strongest ally, Obama gave Prime Minister Brown twenty-five DVDs that Brown could have bought anywhere in the United States or England if he wanted something that frivolous. I will not go into the gifts given to Brown's children because of the Obama's got more thoughtless, cheap, and shabby.

[12] In 2009, following his visit to Saudi Arabia and Egypt, Obama completed his international trip with brief stops in Europe including appearances at Buchenwald with German Chancellor Angela Merker and at the D-Day Memorial with French President Nicolas Sarkozy.

Unfortunately, our relations with Germany were becoming more strained – a tension that dates back to the Presidential Campaign when Merkel rejected Obama's request during the campaign to speak in front of the Brandenburg Gate. During the visit to Buchenwald, Obama appropriately rebuked Holocaust deniers, but also expressed grief and outrage for German actions in World War II – a marked contrast to the understanding message he had recently given to the world's Muslims.

Obama's attitude toward French President Sarkozy was also strained. With ill manners, he shocked both the French and British with his effort to get the Queen of England invited to the weekend's D-Day Memorial. This same day, Obama refused a dinner invitation from Sarkozy and his wife. The U.K. Times speculated that Obama's irritation stems from the previous G2 Summit when, in private, Sarkozy told colleagues that he found Obama to be inexperienced and unbriefed, especially on climate change.

We could cover more examples, but I believe that the foregoing examples are sufficient to show Obama's raging anti-colonialism is as strong as a powerful spotlight on a dark night. These examples show that he is a danger to the United States. However, these examples are tame to what he will eventually do to American and our Washington Establishment politicians of both parties will permit these actions as long as we permit them to remain in office.

Regardless of his multitude of faults, Obama is a very intelligent person, but with some mental flaws. He certainly is not as intelligent as he believes himself to be. This is common with his personality type. Combine intelligence with a devious mind loaded with years of hatred, hardcore radical training and plans for revenge and you then have a strong and dangerous person. Compare Obama with other famous Socialist leaders and you will see many common traits.

Obama does not hesitate to flaunt our Constitution by using schemes to get around it to achieve his goals. He is slick, sly, and relentless in getting what he wants, yet acts like a child when rebuffed.[13] One huge stroke he has taken is the appointment of a huge number of czars – all who have very radical backgrounds. The appointment of czars is considered unconstitutional by many experts but has been used since Franklin D. Roosevelt first used them. Through the following years, probably all presidents have appointed czars in a limited amount, but not to the extent done by Obama. As of my last count,

THE OBAMA TRAGEDY

Obama has appointed more than forty-two and when their backgrounds are checked, it shows that practically all of them are far out radicals who must be considered detrimental to our way of life. The following are a few examples:

1. An admitted former Communist.
2. A far Leftist who wants all guns confiscated and destroyed.
3. A strongly Anti-American and member of a Leftist group in Latin America.
4. A former, corrupt Fannie Mae CEO.
5. One who calls America the meanest and wealthiest of all countries.
6. One who promoted homosexuality in schools.
7. One who wants legal rights for livestock, wildlife, and pets.
8. A left-wing radical who wants Israel split up into two or more smaller, more manageable plots.
9. A well-known Socialist appointed as Administrator of the Center for Medicine.
10. A Leftist who wants rights for terrorists and believes that the U.S. is the cause of world terrorism.
11. A previous university dean who teaches that America caused world poverty, ACORN board member: W.E.B. Dubois (Communist) Club member.

The list goes on and on with individuals of similar backgrounds. Many websites will provide similar lists of these czars, but probably will not provide their backgrounds. If you want to review the above list, which not only provides the backgrounds but also shows their pictures, then go to: theobamafile.com/ObamaCzar.htm.

Another question frequently asked: "Does Barrack Obama have a Narcissistic Personality Disorder?" Psychologists and Psychiatrists have come to the conclusion, without benefit of actual examination. Most feel their conclusions are sufficient and valid through frequent observations since Obama is constantly campaigning under the guise of news conferences and announcements. His manner of speech is very revealing as are many actions that he takes. With these facts at hand, they feel their conclusions are, without a doubt, valid.

What exactly are we talking about when we discuss a Narcissistic Personality Disorder? The following definition comes from an extremely reliable source and is quite interesting. This definition comes from the highly respected Mayo Clinic Staff:

[14] "Narcissistic Personality Disorder is a mental disorder in which people have an inflated sense of their own importance and a deep need for admiration. Those with Narcissistic Personality Disorder believe that [they are] superior to others and have little regard for other people's feelings. But behind this mask of ultra-confidence, lies a fragile self-esteem vulnerable to the slightest criticism."

[15] The Diagnostic and Statistical Manual of Mental Disorders describes narcissism as a personality disorder that revolves around a pattern of grandiosity, a need for admiration, and a sense of entitlement. Often individuals feel overly important and will exaggerate achievements and will accept, and often demand, praise and admiration despite worthy achievements.

[16] The Diagnostic and Statistical Manual of Mental Disorders is published by the American Psychiatric Association. This book is typically considered the "bible" for any professional who makes psychiatric diagnoses in the United States and many other countries.

[17] The causes for Narcissistic Personality Disorder can be traced back to the childhood of the individual suffering from the disorder. By the onset of early adulthood, the trauma experienced in childhood engulfs the mind of the individual. One of the causes is neglect by the parents. In the case of Obama, we know that he was abandoned by his father shortly after birth. He was tossed around, neglected, and eventually abandoned by his mother. Such actions are considered severe neglect and certainly could have had a traumatic effect on him.

[18] In connection with the cause of Narcissistic Personality Disorder, we will look at the first two lists of narcissistic behavior traits or characteristics:

THE OBAMA TRAGEDY

1. Narcissists are hypersensitive to insults, defeat, criticism, and often tend to react aggressively when faced with such situations.
2. They are introverts, hence they do not make it obvious even if they are hurt.
3. They are preoccupied with fantasies related to power, wealth, success, and love.
4. They feel they are special and hence desire to be treated in a special way.
5. They lack the ability to understand human emotions. They do not try to understand other people's needs, feelings, or viewpoints.
6. Narcissists are self-centered and consider themselves to be superior to others.
7. They are boastful and often indulge in exaggerating themselves and their achievements.
8. They set unrealistic goals for themselves and do not hesitate in taking extreme measures to attain these goals.
9. They like being constantly admired and crave to always be the center of attention.
10. They appear very arrogant in nature and sport an unnecessary attitude or ego most of the time.
11. They are always envious about others but simultaneously think that other people are envious of them.

In addition to the above, narcissists are often callous and ruthless. They usually lack a conscience. They lead by words and believe that they can move mountains simply by talking with a glib tongue.

Narcissists are often high achievers despite their personality disorders. They often aspire to reach high leadership positions wherein they can satisfy their exaggerated abilities, receive subservience from others, and can cut loose their callous, ruthless, and dangerous desires.

The following are a few people who had or have Narcissistic Personality Disorders:

1. Napoleon Bonaparte
2. Adolph Hitler
3. Joseph Stalin
4. Franklin D. Roosevelt
5. George Soros
6. Louis Farrakhan

[19] As stated earlier, I am providing another list of characteristics of the narcissist and others with personality disorders. The characteristics apply to both males and females.

1. Self-centered – his needs are paramount.
2. No remorse for mistakes of misdeeds.
3. Unreliable and undependable.
4. Does not care about the consequences of his actions.
5. Projects faults onto others. High blaming behavior – never his fault.
6. Little, if any, conscience.
7. Insensitive to needs and feelings of others.
8. Has a good front (persona) to impress and exploit others.
9. Low stress tolerance. Easy to anger and rage.
10. People are to be manipulated for his needs.
11. Rationalizes easily. Twists conversation to his gain at others' expense. If trapped, keeps talking, changes the subject or gets angry.
12. Pathological lying.
13. Tremendous need to control situation.
14. No real values. Mostly situational.
15. Often perceived as caring and understanding and uses this to manipulate.
16. Angry, mercurial moods.
17. Uses sex to control.
18. Does not share ideas, feelings, and emotions.
19. Conversation controller. Must have the first and last word.

20. Is very slow to forgive others. Hangs onto resentment.
21. Secret life. Hides money, friends, and activities.
22. Likes annoying others. Likes to create chaos and disruption for no reason.
23. Moody – switches from nice guy to anger without much provocation.
24. Repeatedly fails to honor financial obligations.
25. Seldom expresses appreciation.
26. Grandiose. Convinced he knows more than others and is correct in all he does.
27. Lacks ability to see how he comes across to others. Defensive when confronted with his behavior. Never his fault.
28. Can get emotional, tearful. This is about show or frustration rather than sorrow.
29. He breaks women's spirits to keep them dependent.
30. Needs threats and intimidations to keep others close to him.
31. Sabotages partner wants her to be happy only through him and to have few friends.
32. Highly contradictory.
33. Convincing. Must convince people to side with him.
34. Hides his real self.
35. Kind only if he is getting what he wants from you.
36. He has to be right. He has to win. He has to look good.
37. He announces, not discusses. He tells, not asks.
38. Does not discuss openly, has a hidden agenda.
39. Controls money of others but spends freely on himself.
40. Unilateral condition of: "I am okay and justified so I do not need to hear your position or ideas."
41. Always feels misunderstood.
42. You feel miserable with this person. He drains you.
43. Does not listen because he does not care.
44. His feelings are discussed, not the partner's.
45. Is not interested in problem-solving.
46. Very good at reading people, so he can manipulate them.

Sometimes called gas lighting.

I certainly do not pretend to be a Psychologist or Psychiatrist. However, I have studied personality disorders to a good extent. In addition, I have known many narcissists and, as a Battalion Commander in the U.S. Army, I have often worked with mental health professionals in their treatment of soldiers under my command. When asked if I believe Obama is a narcissist, my opinion is definitely yes.

When I combine Obama's many Narcissistic Personality Disorder traits with his life-long associations with Socialists, radicals, terrorists, racists, and his early Islamic training which tends to make him Pro-Muslim and Anti-Israel, I have to do serious thinking. As I think deeper of his anti-colonialism, his manner of speech, his body language, his taking of credit for the accomplishments of others, and his downgrading of America and the Presidency in foreign nations such as the disgusting scene of him bowing down to Arab leaders and apologizes for the actions of the United States – then my mind becomes perfectly clear. In my thought process, this man is extremely dangerous to our American way of life.

CHAPTER **13**

Taking Back America

IN THIS FINAL chapter, I again remind you of The Evil Octopus (The Illuminati/International Bankers) and its nefarious actions which control America. I must also point out that the takeover of the United States could/would not have happened if the citizenry had upheld its responsibility.

There are two imperative questions that we must address as we approach the all important solution of regaining our wonderful country:

1. Why did we allow the wealthiest, strongest, and most important nation known to mankind to fall into the lowly state of a bankrupt nation with an unsustainable debt, and despite recently raising the debt ceiling, our credit rating dropped to the level of the small island of Bermuda?
2. What must we do to get our country back and return it to its lofty status of the past?

It is ironic that one of the things that made America great is probably the main thing that brought about our downfall. American citizens have always been known for their industrious nature, ingenuity, and desire for family and national security. These passions were relatively easy to attain through our free enterprise system. As it always is with human beings, those who worked the hardest and prepared for advancement were the most successful.

God did not make all people equal in many ways. Some are more intelligent than others, some are more gifted, and some are more mechanically inclined, while others are more studious. Then there are those who have lower ambitions, no real desire to succeed, and will gladly live from the labor of others and will eventually believe it is an entitlement. Due to various personal characteristics, we have different classes in our society that are fair and natural.

Each generation wanted a better life for their children than they had received from their parents. Consequently, they worked harder, longer, produced more, attained more, and could provide more in the form of necessities and luxuries. In doing so, they had less time to devote to family, religion, and especially education and politics. They chose to entrust these responsibilities to schools and politicians which has proven to be a disastrous choice. This practice became more prevalent with succeeding generations.

During the past few years, there has been much publicity on the World War II generation. In newspapers, books, and television programs, it is often referred to as "America's Greatest Generation." I was too young for military service but consider myself part of that generation. I agree that the actions of practically all Americans were outstanding throughout this period. And many sacrifices were made.

We were a military force that was ill-prepared and ill-equipped, but soon became the greatest fighting force the world has ever known. I well remember, at age eleven, I began selling newspapers at Camp Toccoa, Georgia where several Airborne Regiments trained for the invasion of Normandy. In fact, I remember during the period of July through December of 1942 that part of my "customers" were Easy Company, five hundred and sixth Airborne Regiment from which the TV movie "Band of Brothers" was made. Going to Camp Toccoa at four in the morning and returning at four in the afternoon, I saw the rigorous training that they received and other hardships that they endured.

Civilians certainly did their share. Dormant manufacturing plants closed during the Great Depression were quickly refurbished and began producing badly needed war equipment and supplies. Women began joining the workforce, filling jobs where no men were available. We endured rationing where many food items were rationed. I remember our family was allowed one pound of coffee per month. We always ran out before our next coupon became valid, so my mother saved the grounds (dregs) and reused them at the end of the month. We were allowed one, possibly two pairs of shoes per year. Meat was very scarce, except Spam, which was usually available. Gasoline was closely rationed. By the end of 1942, more than one-half of automobiles were issued "A" stickers which allowed four gallons of fuel per week. For almost one year, "A" stickered cars were not to be driven for pleasure. A Mileage Ration Book with coupons controlled the usage. Other stickers used such as the "B" stickers for those workers deemed essential to the war effort and they were allowed eight gallons per week. These are just a few of the rationed items, as well as only a few of the sacrifices the American citizen made. Can you imagine how the generation of today would react to such actions? My guess is that there would be massive rioting, looting, and all forms of lawlessness.

Yes! It was a great generation, but it also had its downside and proved to be the accelerator that hastened our downfall from a Constitutional Republic to our current warped, out-of-control government. Many will think this is an absurd statement, therefore an explanation is due.

Many parts of our country had not recovered from the Great Depression until World War II began and after the war was over, the economy boomed. Jobs were readily available and everyone wanted a new home, car, washing machine, stove, refrigerator, and other luxuries for themselves and their children, since none of these luxury items had been manufactured since 1941. With the job market wide open, women began to pour into the workforce and breakdown of the family structure began. The G.I. Bill was available to veterans and masses of young men were earning college degrees of which they otherwise would have never dreamed.

◄ ONCE THERE WAS AN AMERICA

This rush to materialism is maddening. With both parents working, there was loss of parental supervision and children were lavished with everything from toys to automobiles. In order to provide this new lifestyle, parents neglected their civic, religious, and moral responsibilities. Parents were oblivious to what was happening politically, as well as the moral decay of our country. They were just too busy to care. As a result, their children became more disobedient, more promiscuous, and more demanding.

The 1950s were not terribly bad, but we saw the youth of the 1960s and decades beyond go to the extreme socially, politically, morally, and religiously. Many, such as Obama's buddy and terrorist, Bill Ayers, would have gladly fought a more violent revolution. Instead, most of these Anti-American scum bags entered the political arena and even more entered the field of education. In doing so, they adversely altered our laws and warped the minds of our children, which continues to the present time.

As a veteran of the Korean and Viet Nam Wars, it hurts to say this of my fellow veterans of World War II – you made tremendous sacrifices, you were magnificent warriors, you fought and won one hell of war. But after the war was over, you neglected your duty of Citizenship and are partially responsible for the sad state of disarray our country is currently experiencing.

We now move onto the second question, "How do we get our country back?" First, if you believe in God, pray. Next, you must ask yourself if you are willing to exert great effort, make sacrifices, be ridiculed, go to jail, and be subject to physical danger.

True conservative, patriotic citizens must organize into a highly efficient, well-defined movement that surpasses any known political or social organization ever developed. There are thousands of you out there with the appropriate education level, organizational skills, leadership ability, speaking acumen, drive, and patriotism to organize and lead such a movement. **So make up your mind and start moving now.**

I would gladly take on such an endeavor, but I am too darn old. I may have the energy for a period of time, but my remaining years are too few. I will give you some guidance, many suggestions, point out some pitfalls, etc. Actually this book, if every published, was to be my last effort in providing information and guidance to all who were deprived of this knowledge through our education system, our churches, our families, and the mainstream media. The future is now up to you patriots who are brave and willing to work your butts off.

I am to not writing about just one more namby-pamby type of organization that relies on "get out the vote" or "write your Congressman" messages while asking for money. Nor am I writing about so-called conservative organizations that only want to write, publish, and sell books, but do not have the courage to hit the streets. It is too late for this patsy type of paying around. Nor am I writing about a violent, unlawful rebellion; however, after you are well-organized and gain some power, it will be necessary to take it to the streets, which we will discuss later. Although you will not be violent, there probably will be violence put upon you.

The structure of your organization must be built for frequent and rapid response. I will not provide you with a sample organizational chart because you should do that on your own. It may be as simple as a national office followed by regional, state, district, county, and city/town offices. The structure may need to be more complex but the key is to have well-trained and knowledgeable personnel at each office. Example: National Office receives word that Senator Smith is speaking in Kansas City on a proposed conservative bill for tax reform. National notifies State Chairman of Missouri, Kansas, Illinois, Iowa, and Nebraska to have at least five hundred members from each state to be at the event at the designated date, time, and place. Naturally, each State Chairman notifies the District Chairman, he/she notifies the County Chairman, who in turn notifies City/Town. The number of attendees required from each level will be determined by population and distance from the event.

As you see, such an organization can be expanded or contracted as needed. Of course all members of this national organization will be educated as responsible and knowledgeable citizens who follow the existing laws. Their main goal is to return America to its rightful place, a Constitutional Republic with a small representative government, controlled spending via a balanced budget. It will be the Organization's responsibility to educate and elect public officials who believe in this same form of government. Conversely, it is the Organization's responsibility to oppose and defeat those public officials who do not believe in our Constitutional Republic.

I deliberately gave you a view of the type of organization we need before discussing details of how to build from the ground up. It can be done quicker than one may think. A good example is the Tea Party that was loosely organized and came into prominence practically overnight, yet look at the results of the recent mid-term elections with the staggeringly high number of conservatives elected to both houses of Congress. This came about because millions of Americans want our dysfunctional government returned to one that is truly American, not the Socialist debacle of Obama and the Democrats, especially the far left.

Organizing takes money so you have to forcefully go after it. Most of you are adept with computers and the entire social media network. After you have your organization laid out and your initial objectives prioritized, set up a website soliciting donations and annual membership dues at a reasonable dollar amount per year. Do not forget that there are "deep pockets" who favor conservative causes. I will not use names since I have not obtained permission to do so. You will find several by searching with your computer for sites such as "The Billionaires who Support the Tea Party" and "California Conservative Philanthropists." There are many more sites, so just start searching.

Get out! Go to conservative meetings and make contacts, prepare inexpensive but attractive handouts, call in or get on conservative talk shows, send e-mail to these same people or other interested individuals, take advantage of free advertisements such as Public Service Announcements (PSAs), community calendars on local radio and TV stations, hold informational and membership rallies at inexpensive public places like parks, amphitheaters, etc. Use your imagination!

After your war chest has grown, start well-prepared advertisements in appropriate media.

Always remember you are the real Americans. As such, everything you do must be legal. Most, if not all, patriotic beliefs and activities are legal regardless of what the bias and controlled media says. Know what you are talking about before you spout off. Keep your cool when debating individuals in opposition to your views because they are usually well-trained and will talk over you if allowed, will avoid answering direct questions, and will change the subject if trapped. Have facts clearly implanted in your mind in order to tactfully and accurately defend your statements. Your every action must be correct for evil eyes will be upon you.

Of utmost importance is your knowledge of the United States Constitution. That is why I included Chapter Six as a true copy for your use. I deliberately placed it near the center of this book, hoping you would read it. Now you must study it, remember it, and be able to use it. Although too many progressive individuals have been appointed to the Supreme Court and rendered some horrendous opinions, it is still the glue that holds our country together and provides you with protection in the effort to reclaim America.

Take this warning. When you form the organization, you will immediately be infiltrated. This infiltration will come from the United States government and Leftist/Socialist groups as a minimum. Do not be surprised if your most ardent and efficient members turn out to be plants within the organization. They will likely rise to high positions and remain for years. If they are Feds, they will pimp you out to Washington, D.C., but if you are lawful not too much damage will be done unless leaked to the press who will distort what was reported. Agents from Leftist/Socialist groups are quite different, they will leak your plans to try to disrupt your activities. There is a multitude of Leftist/Socialist groups that reach into the hundreds, maybe thousands. They are mostly neglected and allowed to operate as they choose. On the other hand, conservative, patriotic organizations are few and are under almost constant scrutiny and often forced out of existence by government agencies aided by the news media. Since conservatives are true, patriotic Americans, one would think the reverse should be true.

As you prepare your rapid plan of notification to members of meetings, demonstrations, protests, etc., you must have a manual back-up plan in place. Your electronic plan is probably known and can be jammed. There are various ways to create a back-up plan. Cell phones are not as likely jammed as landlines and not as easily monitored. Telegraph messages to key individuals who will disburse the information can be effective. Plan wisely for any possible scenario. Do not forget: "runners" by use of automobiles can also be effective. Remember the strike-breakers from another chapter, who in New York City, had a roster of thirty-five thousand strike-breakers and could assemble several thousand in a matter of hours.

Think big when it comes to membership. Think not in thousands, but in millions. I assure you that they are there if your approach is well-planned as the "American Way," which is sincere, well-defined, and patriotic. Be enthusiastic, but not as raging radicals. Make sure all members are well-trained, strong, and self-disciplined. I will not try to fool you – the odds are stacked against you. You will be fighting the strongest of the strongest, such as the biased and controlled mainstream media, the Council on Foreign Relations, the Trilateral Commission, the American Civil Liberties Union, labor unions, the International Bankers, and elements of the United States government to name a few. However, you can succeed. Be optimistic even in failures, just remember the story of David and Goliath.

Keep in mind that little victories will lead to bigger victories. Initially, you should throw support to lower level offices being pursued by a relatively strong conservative candidate. Do this in several states and use the success as credentials when you up the chain to the higher offices such as senatorial and presidential races. One of your goals is to become so strong that you can swing most elections to the American Way, not the Anti-American, Socialist way we have followed by gradualism and apathy for many past decades.

When you select a candidate to support, go directly to him or her and show your strength and emphasizing how effective you can be in him or her being elected. If the candidate chooses to accept your support, make it conditional that he or she become properly educated. Require that the candidate read this book because all that is contained therein has been verified and was written to get our country back on the right path.

Do not consider forming a third political party. At this time, to do so will only strengthen the Socialist-leaning Democratic Party. Although the Republican Party has its share of Socialists and do nothing, Washington Establishment members in both houses of Congress, they are still the better choice. However, we must turn the Republican Party into a true Conservative Party in order to get our country back. I assure you that it can be done. I again refer you to the recent success of the Tea Party which really is not a political party in the true sense. I have been to three Tea Party rallies and saw good, knowledgeable Americans. I saw no racism, hatred, or violent behavior. In fact, I have seen these types escorted away from the events and later were determined Leftists who were there to make the event look bad. The lead-off speaker for two of these events was a black female. I saw Hispanics, Orientals, and Arabs at each event. I also saw political Independents, Democrats, and Libertarians. So all this deliberate hatred put out by the Democratic Party and the biased media is totally unfounded since I have received similar reports from friends in other states.

The following are some projects on which we, as individual conservatives or member of conservative groups, should begin working on immediately. They are in no particular order of importance, so pick a few and start working on them now:

1. We already know the Federal Reserve System is unconstitutional and should be abolished, but this is so unrealistic to almost all American citizens and incompetent politicians that we most likely cannot get it done. Instead, we must first

educate the public and the ignorant politicians, then strip the Federal Reserve System of the Wall Street/International Bankers, and install clean, independent American bankers with strict Congressional Oversight Rotating Committees with annual audits.

2. Since we are a bankrupt nation, get a copy of the recent report by the General Accounting Office (GAO) which shows many billions of dollars spent on absolutely wasteful items, projects, etc. Then start raising Cain about this absurd waste and demand Congress get it back or stop that which has not yet been spent. This must be followed up with proper controls to prevent this wastefulness which happens every year.

3. Withdraw our funds from the [1] World Bank, the [2] International Monetary Fund, get out of the worthless United Nations for which we have been paying more than twenty-seven percent (now reduced to twenty-two percent – wow!). Combine these and we will save billions.

4. Drastically reduce or stop all foreign aid. We provide the overwhelming majority of it and are hated by those we help.

5. Get our military forces out of Europe. Most are stationed in Germany but we have military personnel in more than forty foreign countries. Let Europe take up the slack if it is necessary. We have many vacant military installations scattered across the U.S. and this will stimulate the local and national economy. These troops could also be deployed along our borders and effectively stop illegal immigration. In essence, it would cost us nothing. Of course, common sense and rational thinking is foreign to our politicians.

6. The number of Federal employees should and easily could be cut by twenty percent and would save billions annually. You would agree with me if you actually saw how little Federal employees accomplish and even most of that is on meaningless projects using poor methods. Do not forget the thirteen or more paid holiday, lengthy vacations, and a lenient sick day

policy. Many have been hired simply as voters for politicians. Obama's stimulus plan produced very few jobs and most were needless Federal employees. [3] Each job created cost two hundred and seventy-eight thousand yet Obama wants more stimulus money for jobs.

7. Something must be done about the mainstream media that presents a one-sided liberal view that is totally unfair and much of it untrue. It will do no good to write a major network so you will have to go to more drastic measures. Document their biased views by comparing them with the balanced network, Fox News, who presents both sides of the issue. During interviews, document the hard and often trick questions asked of conservative guests to the soft, marshmallow questions asked of liberal guests. It may be necessary to start using boycott tactics. It will be more effective to start at the local level by contacting the station manager with the complaint and your intentions to boycott local advertisers and let him notify the network (you should notify advertisers in advance). You may choose to keep a log of large corporate sponsors and notify them of your intentions. Money talks and the loss of it hurts. Of course a protest at national headquarters by several thousand protestors could have a positive effect.

8. Every conservative should immediately start screaming for a [4] Fair Tax Act which would apply a tax once at the point of purchase on all new goods and services for personal consumption. The current proposal also calls for a monthly payment to all family households of lawful U.S. residents as an advance rebate, or "pre-bate" of tax on purchases up to the poverty level. This Act would replace the Internal Revenue Service (think of the billions saved) and all federal income taxes including Social Security and Medicare taxes, capital gains taxes, gift taxes, and estate taxes with a national retail sales tax. There are two bills in Congress introduced earlier this year. [5] H.R. 25 introduced by Rep. Bob Woodall

(Ga.). And [6] S-13 introduced by Republican Senator Saxby Chambliss (Ga.) and co-sponsored by Senator Richard Burr (N.C.), Senator Tom Coburg (OK), Senator Jim DeMint (S.C.), Senator Johnny Isakson (Ga.), and Senator Jerry Moran (Ks).

9. We must begin getting true conservatives into Congress. The recent reclaiming of the House is rewarding and we need to elect more new conservatives to both houses of Congress and get rid of those who are ineffective. The real problem is in the Senate. This will sound drastic but I estimate that no more than twenty-nine percent of our Republican Senators can be called conservative. Few show any leadership ability, they appear to cower to Democrats on most issues, they often vote liberal on matters of importance, they hide behind their desks and do not come out and publicly denounce bad policies, and they fail to propose or fight for meaningful legislation. Some have done practically nothing for two terms or more. Some are simply dumb, lazy, and uninformed. They come to office knowing nothing and do whatever career bureaucrats advise them to do and take initiative to better prepare themselves. We must replace all these types with those of courage, intelligence, and fiery drive.

10. Force Congress to pass a law making earmarks illegal.

11. Do not cut our military strength. It should be doubled as a minimum. In the not too distant future, a war with China is inevitable. Currently, China has an army of more than one million soldiers. They have already boasted that they have a missile delivery system that can reach the West Coast of the United States and are rapidly improving the system. Using our money through debt payments and unfair trade agreements, they are rapidly building aircraft carriers that will bring danger closer to our shores. Ask any combat veteran of the Korean War and he will tell you that the Chinese soldier has a different concept of life than Americans. He will tell you of the horrible sound of thousands of Chinese soldiers, high

on opium, rushing forward at night, screaming and blowing bugles. Despite being mowed down by machine gun fire, they would keep on coming. Do not fool yourself, it can and will happen again. Our present military force is good, but far, far too small and, in a conventional war, cannot handle the Chinese army. Also remember, China has nuclear power and will not hesitate to use it.

I will begin closing this book by making direct comments to individuals and groups. I do especially want to state that this book was written to every American regardless of religion, race, or political persuasion in order to provide you with knowledge of which most of you have been deprived. I would be untruthful if I did not tell you that my hopes are that you will realize the severe danger that we are in as a nation and that our only hope is to follow a conservative path out of the chaotic state that we are in. Yes! I want to convert all who are politically indifferent, moderate, liberal, or any other political persuasion.

To all you Master and PhD degree holders, it will be difficult to accept the information I have presented and you will try to rationalize it away. You are highly intelligent, probably successful, and will find it hard to accept the fact that you are ignorant of what is really happening to our country and the entire world. You will find it equally hard to accept that fact that you were conned by teachers and professors throughout your years of education. I understand this very well because I have sat through many classes, listening to piles of garbage that I knew were absolute lies. Then, I was forced to regurgitate this crap back to liberal professors in order to get the required grade in graduate studies. Now is the time to add to your knowledge and, at the same time, cleanse yourself of the false doctrines imposed upon you.

Be a new person. Get involved in worthwhile conservative causes. Go to Parent/Teacher Organization meetings and help stabilize them for they are often lead by individuals with a liberal, unpatriotic agenda. Get on library committees. Make proper arrangements and frequently sit-in on classes at local schools. If there is a conservative meeting, rally, demonstration, etc., forget your weekend golf game. Your country is more important than playing games.

To you who are even higher educated, the same above comments apply to you. Perhaps you are a MD or DDS with a successful practice and have seen from twenty to sixty patients today, but there is a meeting of the Board of Education and you are just too tired to go. Get up! Go to the meeting because they are deciding what textbooks are to be used in the coming year. Currently, there are hundreds of textbooks that are completely inappropriate and you need to protest their use. This is just one of many actions you need to be involved with in order to protect your children and the country that gave you an abundant life.

There are many other groups who need to make some small sacrifices and get involved in your patriotic duties. Remember, patriotism also means a certain amount of Conservatism. This means you wild, partying college students must not swallow the Socialist slop you are being fed in the classroom. It also means to cut some of your party time and work for patriotic causes. You macho-talking guys, who hang out and talk big in sports bars, show how tough you are by studying a bit and joining some patriotic demonstrations and rallies, else you may not have a bar to brag in. You gang members get off the streets and quit sucking up to your leaders who are only punks who are conning you. The same applies to you young men who belong to hate groups like the New Black Panthers Party or the Ku Klux Klan. Get with us and stop being duped into making money for and building a false power base for your leaders.

We will now take a look at the churches and religion, keeping in mind that not all church goers are religious and some churches preach and teach false doctrines. [7] Most major research firms conclude that church goers comprise of about forty-nine percent of the United States population. More recent researchers believe a more accurate figure is twenty-six percent. Several reasons are attributed to this difference, to include people who give false information, answer the way in which they think the researcher wants them to, and the manner in which the question is asked. Regardless of which number you choose, it shows the clergy and church members are doing an extremely poor job in one of their prime duties.

I have much to say on the subject of religion and the responsibilities of believers, their leaders and their institutions. The Clergy, Theologians, and Biblical Scholars will come up with a multitude of reasons, studies, scripture passages, etc. to prove me wrong. In the final analysis, their efforts will mean nothing because a good, simple, and truthful answer to specific problems is correct. Since I am of the Christian Faith, my remarks will be from that viewpoint. However, I believe my remarks apply to all faiths and religions. And yes, Virginia! Catholics are Christians.

I firmly believe that God gave us this grand and glorious country. I know our wonderful Constitution was written as the Holy Bible being used as a guide by our founding fathers. Accordingly, one of the most important requirements of a Christian is civic responsibility. For many decades, Christians and the clergy have progressively become more negligent in this duty. It has become easy to use the phrase "Separation of Church and State" as a cop out. The clergy is probably more guilty than their followers in using this cop out because it takes less effort to be passive than try to approach a controversial subject. Civic responsibility is the same as evangelism and without doubt should be included in the teaching ministry of the church.

The First Amendment to the Constitution is clear and simple, and states, "Congress shall make no law respecting an establishment of religion, or prohibiting the free exercise thereof." This simply means that there is to be no state religion imposed upon citizens, but it also encourages us to exercise the freedom of religion and create our own churches. As we well know, activist judges have bastardized this Amendment to the ridiculous extent that we can no longer have non-denominational prayer or Biblical readings in the classrooms, no prayer by students at athletic events, graduation ceremonies, etc.

In addition, the Ten Commandments cannot be displayed in various public buildings and classrooms. Instead of rising up against such foolish actions, our clergy and church members sat on their lazy behinds and, like sheep, did not say a word. Do not we have great church leaders?

The foregoing does not keep the church from doing some things, if the clergy and church members would not chicken out. Places of worship can distribute voter guidelines, run non-partisan voter registration drives, and hold forums and discussions on matters of public interest – this can include the backgrounds and political persuasions of candidates. The things that the churches are not allowed to do are few. They cannot endorse a candidate and their political activity cannot be biased for or against a candidate, directly or indirectly. White churches are either too stupid or too scared to exercise their rights. Black churches and leaders are much smarter and have been using their churches as centers of political activity since the end of the War Between the States.

In addition, in respect to the actions allowed within the place of worship, church members can do anything that other citizens are allowed to do. In fact, the clergy can encourage their congregations to participate as individuals (no church signs or posters) with conservative groups in various activities like marches, protests, demonstrations, etc. In this way, they are doing their civic duty while at the same time meeting their religious obligation.

It is time for Christians and other religions to get their lazy rear ends off the pews and from the pulpit and hit the streets with those of us who love God and our country and want to take it back. With the massive number of church members combine with various conservative groups, we could surround State Capitols and the National Capitol for two or three consecutive weekends and I assure you that our demands would be met. I well realize that the majority of church congregations are not youngsters, but if seventy-five year olds can take a weeklong church sponsored bus trip, they can participate in a two or three day demonstration – I know, I am eighty.

Church members must take the initiative within the place of worship. Members of the clergy have their own agenda. Some have been brainwashed and will not want to participate. Others have a desire to participate but do not come forth because of fear. In practically all churches where a clergyman/woman would suggest such an idea, the congregation would be so outraged that he or she would be fired within two days. Why? Because most so-called Christians and other religious persons feel comfortable sitting in churches saying, "Glory, I am saved," and do not want to put forth any other effort. Again religious people, I say get involved. Remember your duty to God is to fulfill your public and civic responsibility or someday you may wake up and find you do not have a church. So, get together and, as a group, tell your pastor, priest, or rabbi that the church is going to be publically involved and you expect them to lead the charge.

As a Southern Baptist, I can almost hear the ministers and church members saying, "What will the Southern Baptist Convention say?" Answer – who cares? Such organizations of all faiths are primarily organizations of big business. They take your money and spend billions of dollars printing vast amounts of literature which they sell back to church members. Many invest in properties, stocks, bonds, etc. to show how well the organization is being run. I firmly believe that their leaders have long forgotten that which Christianity is supposed to be. As a result, they have become power-seeking politicians within the church who are satisfying their superegos by attaining the higher positions within the church.

Although churches have their shortcomings, I recommend that everyone become involved with a mainstream denomination. You do not have to be a holy roller and you will find a bit of peace and comfort by attending. After a few times, you will find that it is worth getting up an hour or two earlier than you normally would do. If the church gives you nothing else, it will provide you with a good moral compass.

We could continue with many more organizations and groups who need to become involved, but I will close the subject by saying that the Conservative tent is big enough for everyone regardless of religious beliefs, race, and past affiliations.

As I said much earlier, there is an abundance of individuals who are capable of creating the type of conservative organization that I have tried to convey in this writing. If you will come together, work diligently, and be forceful, fearless, and totally committed to getting our country back, I am sure you will succeed.

We must not make the mistakes of the past. Everyone must have equal opportunity; racism must be reduced to a minimum. Since we are a free enterprise country, some will prosper more than others, but with a "fair tax" system in place, a responsible Congress who will control wasteful spending, a Congressional law prohibiting earmarks, and most all, a balanced budget amendment, everyone should live well. Those who are physically and mentally capable of working must do so and there should be no redistribution of wealth.

I hope you enjoyed and learned from this book and may God be with you in every step that you take.

Notes

CHAPTER 1
1. Webster's Universal College Dictionary
2. Wikipedia.org/wiki/Adam Weishaupt
3. Ibid.
4. Ibid.
5. Guy Carr, Pawns In the Game (1954-55)
6. Wikipedia.org/wiki/Mayer Amschel Rothschild
7. Des Griffin, Descent Into Slavery

CHAPTER 2
1. History @ Kuhnloeb.com
2. Tony D'urso, From Revolution to Reconstruction
3. Civilwarhome.com/europeancivilwar.htm
   Historykb.com/.../580/Russian-navy-during-us-civil-war
4. Izola Forrester, Wikipedia, the free encyclopedia
5. Ibid.
6. Minneapolisfed.org
7. Ibid.
8. 21stcenturycicero.org
9. Ibid.
10. Minneapolisfed.org
11. Answers.com
12. Kuhnloeb.com
13. Answers.com

14. En.wikipedia.org/Jacob Schiff
15. En.wikipedia.org/ Paul Warburg

CHAPTER 3
1. Kuhnloeb.com
2. Eustance Mullins, Secrets of the Federal Reserve
3. Ibid.
4. Ibid.
5. Ibid.
6. Ibid.
7. Ibid.
8. Wikipedia.org/wiki/Federal Reserve Act
9. The Constitution of the United States, Article 1, Section 8, paragraph 5
10. The Structure of the Federal Reserve System,federalreserve.gov/pubs/fresrie/frseri.htm
11. Ibid.
12. Federal Reserve System Audits:Restrictions on GAO access. gao.gov/products/T-GGO-94-44.
13. Answers.com-is the federal reserve federal
14. Globalresearch.com/PHP
15. Overview of the Federal Reserve System, wfhummel-en-chise.comfedoverview

CHAPTER 4
1. David L. Benden, Immigration-Opposing Viewpoints, Chapter 4, page 186
2. Us. History.wisc.edu/hist 102/lecture 08.html
3. Eveioitnesstohistory.com/snpim/.htm
4. En. Wikipedia.org/wiki/Haymarket_Affair
5. Us. History. wisc.edu/hist 102/lecture 08.html
6. En. Wikipedia.org/wiki/Emergency_Quota_Act_of_1924
7. Absoluteastronomy.com/topics/Immigration_Act_of_1924
8. En. Wikipedia.org/wiki/

NOTES

Immigration_and_National_Act_of_1952
9. Thenagain.info/Weeclorn/USA/Immigration Act.htm
10. Gerald Leinenand, American Immigration, page 47
11. The Gale Group, page 43-44, Illegal Immigration
12. Ibid.
13. Infoplease.com/CE6/history/A08498.htm
14. En. Wikipedia.org/wiki/Wagner_Act
15. Answers.com/topic/Danbury-hatters-case
16. Cas.org/news events/connection/hatters.htm
17. Suite 101.com/content/labor-movement-a 75780
18. Jeremy Beecher, Strike, page 301, South End Press
19. En. Wikipedia.org/wiki/Communists_in_the_U.S._Labor Movement
20. En. Wikipedia.org/wiki/TUEL
21. En. Wikipedia.org/wiki/Brookwood_Labor_College
22. En. Wikipedia.org/wiki/Garland_Fund
23. En. Wikipedia.org/wiki/American_Workers_Party
24. Robert H. Ziegler and Gilbert J. Gall, American Workers, American Unions, Third Edition, John Hopkins University Press, page 174
25. Ibid.
26. Gloria Skurzynoki, Sweat and Blood, A History of Labor Unions

CHAPTER 5
1. En. Wikipedia.org/wiki/American_Civil_Liberties_Union
2. Dianedew.com/aclu
3. People downstuff.com/aclu 1.htm
4. En. Wikipedia/org/wiki/Roger_Nash_Baldwin
5. Stoptheaclu.com/2005/12/American-communist-lawyers/
6. Ibid.
7. En. Wikipedia.org/wiki/Lush_Committee
8. David Emerson Gummier, page 15, The ACLU Lawyers Playing the Red Game, American Opinion Books

9. En. Wikipedia.org/wiki/1122_Bridgman_Convention
10. Absoluteastronomy.com/topic/House_Un_American_Activities
11. David Emerson Gummier, page 17, The ACLU Lawyers Playing the Red Hame, American Opinion Books
12. Ibid.
13. En. Wikipedia.org/wiki/American_Civil_Liberties_Union
14. Dianedew.com/aclu.htm

CHAPTER 6
1. JBS Books, P.O. Box 8040, Appleton, Wisconsin 54912
2. House.gov/house/Constitution/Constitution.html
3. House.gov/house/Constitution/Amend.html

CHAPTER 7
1. Conservapedia.com/Socialism
2. En. Wikipedia.org/wiki/European_Union
3. Conservapedia.com/Socialism
4. Charles Krauthamer, Augusta (Ga) Chronicle, June 20, 2011
5. Conservapedia.com/Socialism
6. Conservapedia.com/Similitaries_Between_Communism_Nazism_and_Liberalism
7. Thegalewaypundit.com/2010/08/american-socialist-names-70-cong
8. Wnd.com/3 page=191609
9. En. Wikipedia.org/wiki/Congressional_Progressive_Caucus
10. Bermudaradical.blogspot.com/2008/11/leftist/parites-and-organizations

CHAPTER 8
1. Discoverthenetworks.org/view/Sub Category.asp? Id=217
2. Americanthink.com/2010/02/why_tenureharmes_educatio.html
3. Eagleforum.org/elevate/2001/sept/socialism.html

NOTES

4. Ibid.
5. Ibid.
6. En. Wikipedia.org/wiki/American_Federation_of_Teachers
7. Ibid.
8. Ibid.
9. Wnd.com"paged=114881
10. Examiner.com/Christian-perspectives-in-san-Jose/nea-reveals-a-new-word
11. En. Wikipedia.org/wiki/National_Education_Association
12. Afterexposed.com/tactics

CHAPTER 9
1. En. Wikipedia.org/wiki/Council_on_Foreign_Relations
2. Councilonforeignrelations.net/
3. Ibid.
4. En. Wikipedia.org/wiki/Council_on_Foreign_Relations
5. Councilonforeignrelations.net/
6. En. Wikipedia.org/wiki/Council_on_Foreign_Relations

CHAPTER 10
1. En. Wikipedia.org/wiki/David_Rockefeller
2. Ibid.
3. En. Wikipedia.org/wiki/Trilateral_Commission
4. Afrgen.com/trilateral.htm
5. Councilonforeignrelations.net/
6. En. Wikipedia.org/wiki/Trilateral_Commission
7. Ibid.
8. Ibid.

CHAPTER 11
1. En. Wikipedia.org/wiki/United_Nations
2. En. Wikipedia.org/wiki/United_States_withdrawal_from_the_
3. Betterworldcampaign.org/issues/United_Nations funding/us/dues-and-contributions.htm

4. Un.org/en/peacekeeping/operations/financing/html
5. Answers.yahoo.com/question/index? Gid=2009061172003 AAB doi A
6. Foreignaffairs.com/articles/55875/max-boot/paving-the-road-to-hell-the-failure
7. Answers.yahoo.com/index? Gid=200906151192 003 AABdci AA
8. Reuters, 1 Oct 2010
9. En. Wikipedia.org/wiki/Srebrenia_Massacre
10. Americaresearch.org/biasbasics/biasbasics3.
11. Answers.yahoo.com/questions/index? Gid=2011001071745 AA is Gn
12. En. Wikipedia.org/wiki/Media_bias
13. Mediaresearch.org/biasbasics1.
14. Tdlm.org/News8/Media Leans Left.htm
15. Rense.com/general 144/sevenjewishamericans.htm
16. Ibid.

CHAPTER 12

1. En. Wikipedia.org/wiki/Early_life_and_career_of_Barrack_Obama
2. Associatedcontent.com/article/661873/barrack_obama_admits_past_drug_use.htm
3. Aim.org/aim.com/obama-mentor/
4. Americanthinker.com/blog/2010/obama_radical_associations_at.html
5. Ibid.
6. Jack Kelly, Pittsburgh Post-Gazette, Oct 12, 2008
7. Abcnews.go.com/Blatter/Democratic debate/story? Id=4437888 & page/=/
8. Articles.enn.com/2008/01-07/politics ring. Obama-relatives__sara onyongo=obama---
9. Spectator.org/archives/2008/10/10/Obama-farrakhan-problem

10. Crossroad. To/Quotes/Communism/Alinksy.htm
11. Patterico.com/2008/o6/05/obama-strained-european-relations/
12. Ibid.
13. Theobamafile.com.Obama Czars.htm
14. Mayoclinic.com/health/narcissistic-personality-disorder/0500652
15. The Diagnostic and Statistical Manual for Mental Disorders, Volume 4
16. Allpsy.com/disorders/dsm.htm
17. Buzzle.com/articles/narcissistic-behavior.htm
18. Ibid.
19. Narcissisticabuse.com/characteristics.htm

CHAPTER 13

1. Neseonline.org/NLE/CrS reports/international/inter-51.CFM
2. Ibid.
3. Rep. Kevin McCarthy, Shaun Hannity Show, July 21, 2011
4. En. Wikipedia.org/wiki/Predicted_effects_of_the_Fair_Tax
5. Thomas.loc.gov/czi-bdquery/zid112:HRoo25:
6. Fairtaxnation.com/forum/topics/S13-bill-by-saxby
7. Orthodoxytoday.org/TaylorChurch.php

CPSIA information can be obtained at www.ICGtesting.com
Printed in the USA
LVOW061800250812

295855LV00002B/9/P